Corporate
Social
Accounting

Corporate Social Accounting

Ralph Estes

Elmer Fox Professor of Accounting
Wichita State University

John W. Buckley, Consulting Editor

A Wiley-Interscience Publication

JOHN WILEY & SONS New York / London / Sydney / Toronto

Copyright © 1976 by John Wiley & Sons, Inc.

All rights reserved. Published simultaneously in Canada.

No part of this book may be reproduced by any means,
nor transmitted, nor translated into a machine language
without the written permission of the publisher.

Library of Congress Cataloging in Publication Data:

Estes, Ralph W.
    Corporate social accounting.

    "A Wiley-Interscience publication."
    1. Industry—Social aspects.   2. Cost effectiveness.
I. Title.

HD60.E78   658.4′08   75-42445
ISBN 0-471-24592-5
Printed in the United States of America

10 9 8 7 6 5 4 3 2 1

*Practical men, who believe themselves to be
quite exempt from any intellectual
influences, are usually the slaves of some
defunct economist.*

John Maynard Keynes, *The General
Theory of Employment, Interest
and Money*

Preface

- What is the worth of corporate "social responsibility" activities such as aid to minority business, recycling programs, energy conservation, and participation in the National Alliance of Businessmen?
- Since social responsibility shows up in costs but not in revenues, how can the socially responsible corporation come out as good on the "bottom line" as its irresponsible competitor? How can a company tell the story of its social contribution to the public?
- Will pollution control laws, by driving productive corporations out of business, cost society more than they save?
- How can we measure the value of such things as air pollution, discrimination, consumers' surplus, and industrial accidents? What, for example, is a life worth?
- Should Congress have "bailed out" Lockheed Aircraft? What about New York City?

Social accounting can help provide answers to questions like these—if one has the time to search out and wade through the mass of sometimes conflicting and often confusing material on the subject. This book is an attempt to provide an overview of social accounting as it has been and may be applied in corporations, whether profit seeking or not for profit. The ideas and techniques are also relevant to governmental institutions and noncorporate organizations.

v

Few agree on the meaning of social accounting. This book adopts a broad view that encompasses internal efforts to measure and evaluate the effects on society of socially oriented programs, as well as external reporting on the impact of the corporation and its activities.

The demand for corporate social accounting is large and growing, and it comes as much from the heart of the business world as from citizen groups and government agencies. The first three chapters cover the nature and extent of this demand as well as the responses and experiences of several corporations. Chapter 4 presents an original and comprehensive social accounting model that can be applied to any entity—business firm, hospital, school, church, foundation, government agency or program—to determine the net contribution of that entity to society through an analysis of its social benefits and social costs.

The difficult and critical measurement question is then considered at length, and proven techniques for estimating the dollar values of specific social benefits and costs are presented. These are illustrated with a number of case experiences and research results.

In an effort to bring some order to the anarchic pattern of social reporting, a set of reporting standards is proposed. Among other things, these would require that corporations issuing social reports disclose the bad along with the good.

The book concludes with a step-by-step guide for performing a social accounting. This guide should enable the reader to "get on the learning curve" in undertaking a social performance evaluation of his or her own organization.

Although *Corporate Social Accounting* was written primarily for corporate managers and professional accountants, I hope it will prove to be interesting and useful to anyone interested in this exciting and perplexing new art. Students in particular should benefit from a study of this material, for the future demands for social accounting must ultimately be met by them.

No universally applicable blueprint for social accounting can be offered. The needs of corporate management and of society are too poorly defined, and the circumstances of individual corporations too diverse. But *Corporate Social Accounting* should provide a good start for developing a social accounting program tailored to the needs of a particular organization.

A number of people have influenced this book and the ideas in it, but day in and day out I've gotten more good ideas and had more wrong ones fixed by Sue Estes, my best friend. It is also a pleasure to acknowledge the suggestions and stimulation of John Buckley and David Linowes, and the support of the Elmer Fox Foundation. John Crain of the Wiley organization has courage and style, and seems to get an obscene amount of fun out of his work; it has been a pleasure working with him.

More than anyone else Lee Seidler must bear the blame for first pushing me into social accounting and periodically shoving me along. His debt to society is immeasurable.

Ralph Estes

Wichita, Kansas
December 1975

Contents

1 Social Accounting: What Is It—And Who Cares?   1

2 Corporate Social Accounting: The State of the Art   23

3 Proposed Approaches to Corporate Social Accounting   58

4 A Comprehensive Social Accounting Model   91

5 Social Measurement: Approaches and Cases   108

6 Standards for Corporate Social Reporting   150

7 Now What Are You Going To Do About It?   157

Index   163

An objective of financial statements is to report on those activities of the enterprise affecting society which can be determined and described or measured and which are important to the role of the enterprise in its social environment.

Report of the AICPA Study Group on the Objectives of Financial Statements, October 1973.

1 Social Accounting: What Is It—and Who Cares?

We are in the midst of a social and economic revolution.

The large business firm, once looked upon as the exclusive concern of its owners, is coming to be viewed as an instrument of society. Managers are discovering that maximization of return to stockholders is not a sufficient goal; society is demanding more, and making its demands stick through legislation, litigation, and public pressure. Corporations are being told: "Your job is to serve society through reliable and safe products of high quality. And we expect you to be a good citizen while you're about it—no pollution, no discrimination, no hazardous working conditions. Furthermore, some of your vast economic power should be devoted to social programs. If you can make a good profit too, okay, but these demands come first." The role of the corporation in society is changing dramatically.

The corporate executive is under the gun. He finds it difficult to accept society's growing demands and reconcile them with his traditional view of the corporation. Nevertheless, though sometimes confused and sometimes angered, he has tried to respond in a responsible way.

And in trying to respond the executive has encountered another obstacle: he has discovered that it is at best difficult—often impossible—to get a fix on what his company is doing in terms of social programs and social responsibility.

While the executive has been discovering that he needs some sort of social performance report, so has society—or at least certain important and highly

1

visible elements of society. Congress has repeatedly recognized a need for social performance information in dealing with legislation concerning pollution, mining, and the energy crisis; and with the problems of such corporations as Penn Central, Lockheed Aircraft, and Pan Am. State legislatures, city governments, utility regulatory boards, and a host of public interest groups are recognizing that efficient and equitable allocation of society's resources cannot be made without more information about a corporation and its effects on society.

A substantial amount of information is already available. The public has access to the corporation's annual reports, news releases and news stories, and SEC filings, as well as personal observation and inquiry. Within the corporation the executive has access to information gathered in connection with such required reports as the Equal Employment Opportunity Commission's Form EEO-1, HEW's Form 102, which is mandated by the Occupational Health and Safety Act, and various tax returns. But this isn't enough.

Present reports, especially those made public, emphasize financial information. The typical corporate information system is designed to gather, process, and report financial results and operating statistics with no regard to other social performance information. The social responsibility movement started over ten years ago (at least in its present incarnation) and business has moved to meet it, but the social accounting that must follow if rational decisions are to be made is only a topic of curious conversation in many corporations. (There are notable exceptions; these are discussed in some detail in Chapter 2.)

Serious concern with corporate social accounting developed in the early 1970s. Because its advocates were responding to a variety of needs, they began to develop information and reports dealing with such issues as the following:

1. Effects of corporate social programs, including charitable contributions, purchasing from minority enterprises and advisory assistance to such businesses, executive staff loans to minority firms and government agencies, beautification programs such as landscaping and tree planting, and sponsorship of youth programs such as the Boy Scouts and Junior Achievement.
2. Corporate performance in hiring and promoting minorities and women.
3. Corporate-generated pollution and pollution control efforts.
4. Illegal campaign contributions.
5. Energy usage and conservation efforts.
6. Consumer issues, including warranties, product safety, and effects of products on the environment.

Socioeconomic accounting, social accounting, social responsibility accounting, social audit—these are some of the names that have been used to describe the new information. This book uses the term *social accounting,* which is defined as follows:

The measurement and reporting, internal or external, of information concerning the impact of an entity and its activities on society.

The scope of social accounting thus includes but extends beyond that of traditionally reported economic effects. A firm may be said to be engaged in social accounting when it moves beyond its financial operations and begins to measure and evaluate its other effects on society.

With this introduction we can now look more closely at the audience for social accounting information—who wants it and why.

THE NEED AND DEMAND FOR SOCIAL ACCOUNTING

Internal Demand

Potential users of corporate social performance information are listed in Exhibit 1-1. This list is representative, but it is not and can never be complete; as with traditional financial information, we can never know all the possible audiences.

Within the corporation the greatest need and the greatest demand come from top management. Top management, especially the chief executive officer, needs social performance information to respond to a critical press, to testify knowledgeably when called on by Congressional committees (as several American oil companies were during the winter fuel crisis of 1973), to answer proxy challenges and stockholders' questions, and to ensure that company policies are followed. The surprise and frustration of top executives at being unable to obtain desired social performance information has been repeated in company after company—and it has too frequently been matched with a similar reaction at discovering that mandated corporate policy regarding social responsibility issues was being subverted or ignored in divisions and subsidiaries.

Corporate directors, especially because of their growing legal liability, need to know in some detail what sort of social programs the company is running

EXHIBIT 1-1 Potential Users of Corporate Social Performance Information

Internal		
Directors	Other employees	Public relations department
Management	Union local	Law department

External

Associated

Investors and lenders—especially churches, foundations, banks, insurance companies, universities, and mutual funds
Customers
Suppliers

Government

Securities and Exchange Commission
Environmental Protection Agency
Equal Employment Opportunity Commission
Department of Housing & Urban Development
Internal Revenue Service
General Accounting Office
Congress, state legislatures, city commissions
Law enforcement agencies
Regulatory agencies and commissions at all levels (FTC, FCC, ICC, etc.)

Public Interest Groups

Project on Corporate Responsibility
Council on Economic Priorities
Accountants for the Public Interest
Corporate Accountability Research Group
Agribusiness Accountability Project
Investor Responsibility Research Center
American Civil Liberties Union
San Francisco Consumer Action
National Affiliation of Concerned Business
   Students

Council for Corporate Review
Citizens Action Program
Tax Action Group
Common Cause
Public Citizen, Inc.
NAACP
Public Communication, Inc.
Sierra Club
Wilderness Society
Friends of the Earth

Others

News media
Stock exchanges
American Institute of Certified Public
   Accountants
American Accounting Association
National Association of Accountants

Financial Analysts Federation
Researchers
Educators
Students and other potential employees
General public

4

and what results it is getting. Directors also need complete information about the effects of the corporation on society; it is probably more important that they be fully informed as to *negative* effects, since this is where the criticism will be directed and this is where the directors may have to defend themselves in court.

General Motors' troubles at its Lordstown plant illustrate how unhappy employees can cost a company directly; while leaks by dissident employees to competitors, government investigators, and public interest groups can result in substantial indirect costs. Employees of major companies have indeed shown a great willingness to talk about company matters to Alice Tepper Marlin's Council on Economic Priorities, Ralph Nader's Corporate Accountability Research Group, and such muckraking columnists as Jack Anderson. Employees want to feel that they are performing responsible work for a responsible company. When this feeling is lost, turnover may increase, productivity may drop, and corporate secrets may turn up in the morning paper. It is not surprising that large corporations like Bank of America and Quaker Oats have directed social performance reports at employees.

Unions can also be expected to seek social performance information. The Oil, Chemical and Atomic Workers' 1973 strike against Shell Oil Company, for example, was partially over a demand for disclosure to employees of the results of industrial health surveys. In a significant merger of interests many of the country's big environmental action groups supported the union, contending that they "should be entitled to participate in decisions to control industrial pollution."[1]

External Demand

The external demand for social accounting information is even more diverse. Stockholders are demanding disclosure and threatening proxy challenges to get it.

> . . . such corporate giants as General Motors and Xerox have given in to threats by dissident shareholders rather than see the challenges put to a vote at their annual meetings. Faced with the threat of a proxy challenge, each has agreed to disclose information about minority and women's hiring practices.[2]

---

1 *Business Week,* February 24, 1973, p. 86.
2 *Business Week,* April 13, 1974, p. 89.

Most of these demands—at least those likely to have a real impact—are coming from the large institutional investors: churches, foundations, universities, insurance companies, banks, and mutual funds.

Religious organizations were among the first institutions to call for an accounting for corporate social behavior. Church influence and investor power are illustrated by the following groups:

1. The National Council of Churches' Corporate Information Center evaluates corporations in five areas: the environment; consumer health, welfare, and safety; foreign investment; military production and procurement; and minorities and women.

2. The Center for Social Action of the United Church of Christ has filed several shareholder proposals.[3] The Church's report *Investing Church Funds for Maximum Social Impact* makes the following recommendations with respect to the restricted and unrestricted funds (in excess of $200 million) invested by the Church:

    a. Cash balances should be considered for deposit in minority-group ownership banks.

    b. Instrumentalities and Conferences should actively seek involvement to achieve socially beneficial change in corporate practice through their ownership of stock in such corporations.

    c. Instrumentalities and Conferences are urged to commend, privately and publicly, corporations which take steps to make socially beneficial changes.

    d. All Instrumentalities and Conferences are urged to consider, as a fundamental guide to investment of their restricted dollars, corporations which, by their activity and product as well as their management policy, offer social benefit to the community.

    e. The securities of those corporations engaged in business activities in emerging nations which support oppression of minority groups, where profit-making by cheap labor is a factor, or which support a program of discrimination in employment, should be regarded as least worthy of the investment of church-related dollars.

    f. All Instrumentalities and Conferences are urged to seriously consider the investment of a substantial portion, not less than ten percent, of their unrestricted funds in high-risk and low-return—but maximum social im-

---

3 *Business Week*, April 13, 1974, p. 89.

pact—investments, where the purpose is consistent with their charter provisions.[4]

3. A division of the American Baptist Convention recently sold $641,000 of United Aircraft Corporation stock because it objected to the amount of military business done by United.[5] And the American Baptist Board of Education and Publication, with a coalition of Protestant churches in a "Church Project on U.S. Investments in Southern Africa," recently presented a proxy proposal calling for a detailed report on First National City Corporation's involvement in the Republic of South Africa. (The proposal drew less than 1% support from Citicorp shareholders, however.)[6]

4. The Clergy and Laity Concerned, a New York-based nondenominational peace group, and the National Federation of Priests' Councils, representing 131 priests' councils around the country, have submitted proxy proposals to both Exxon and General Electric calling for reports on military contract work and for the creation of committees to convert defense production to civilian-oriented production.[7]

5. The Interfaith Center for Corporate Responsibility coordinates the activities of some 17 church groups; its executive director argues: "The church is the institution in society that ought to be raising moral and ethical questions because it is outside the economy."[8]

Although they have been understandably hesitant, foundations are also beginning to impose social responsibility criteria on investments and to vote shares in accordance with such standards. The Field Foundation was one of the first foundations to move forthrightly in challenging a company when it submitted three proxy proposals to the Pittston Company in 1973. These proposals called for (1) periodic reporting on Pittston's compensation of victims of a flood caused by collapse of a dam owned by the company, (2) creation of a public policy committee to work on mine safety and ecology measures, and (3) reporting to all shareholders on the proceedings of each annual meeting.[9] The Glide Foundation has filed resolutions with several large corporations calling for dis-

---

4 *Investing Church Funds for Maximum Social Impact* (Report of the Committee on Financial Investments, United Church of Christ, 1970), pp. 50–51.
5 *Fort Worth Star-Telegram,* August 16, 1973.
6 *Business Week,* March 31, 1973, p. 76.
7 *Ibid.,* pp. 76–77.
8 *Business Week,* April 13, 1974, p. 89.
9 *Business Week,* March 31, 1973, p. 78.

closure of minority hiring and promotion data. And the Ford Foundation dispatched an investment officer as an observer to the California CPA Foundation's 1973 Symposium on Measurement of Corporate Social Performance, although whether this presages imposition of social responsibility criteria on investments can only be speculated.

Large universities make very substantial investments, and many are seeking social performance information as a routine part of the evaluation process. Recognizing the inefficiency of each institution independently gathering and analyzing the same information, Harvard's president instigated the formation of the Investor Responsibility Research Center, Inc. The IRRC, which monitors major issues confronting corporations, has grown from 45 clients in 1973 to 90 in 1974. Initially its clientele was largely composed of universities and foundations, but it now includes a number of insurance companies and banks.[10]

Churches, foundations, universities—these are all not-for-profit organizations that might be able to afford the luxury of a lower return on investments in order to meet social performance standards. But what about profit-seeking companies? The big profit-seeking institutional investors—banks, insurance companies, and mutual funds—also appear to be moving in the direction of imposing social performance standards on investments.

Some of the largest banks in the United States, including Bank of America, First National City Bank, and Morgan Guaranty Trust have either "voted proxies against management for social ends or have established high-level committees empowered to recommend such votes."[11] First National City Bank now weighs investments on a social responsibility basis as well as on traditional factors.[12] A number of large life insurance companies are also actively voting their portfolios to achieve social ends. Aetna Life & Casualty, for example, which has $1.5 billion invested in common stocks, voted against management on proxy proposals four times in 1973,[13] and the Institute of Life Insurance has established a Clearinghouse on Corporate Social Responsibility and has called for its members to report on selected social responsibility areas.

"Traditional" mutual funds undoubtedly consider social performance either explicitly or, more likely, implicitly in evaluating their portfolios, but they have

---

10 *Business Week*, April 13, 1974, p. 89.
11 *Business Week*, January 19, 1974, p. 66.
12 *News Front*, January–February 1973, p. 14.
13 The four resolutions called for disclosing of business activities in South Africa, ending investment in the South African territory of Namibia, publicizing political contributions and lobbying, and hiring an outside auditor. See *Business Week*, January 19, 1974, p. 66.

not yet taken an activist role. The demand for social accounting information comes instead from the several new funds that have been created with specific social performance goals in mind; these include The Dreyfus Third Century Fund, First Spectrum Fund, Pax World Fund, and Social Dimensions Fund.

The range of information desired is indicated in the funds' prospectuses. The Dreyfus Third Century Fund, for example, is described as a mutual fund that seeks capital growth through investment in companies showing evidence "of contributing to the enhancement of the quality of life in America." The prospectus further notes:

> The Manager, initially guided by legal requirements which prescribe standards of commercial and social conduct in the areas of concern to the Fund, has developed, and is continuing to develop, techniques for measuring relative performance in these areas of special concern. . . . Currently, development of these techniques and evaluation of companies with respect to these areas are the responsibility of a full-time special research staff of the Manager.[14]

The Fund assesses social performance in four areas: (1) protection and improvement of the environment and the proper use of natural resources; (2) occupational health and safety; (3) consumer protection and product purity; and (4) equal employment opportunity.

First Spectrum Fund evaluates prospective investments with respect to matters involving the environment; employment, civil, and other human rights; and the protection of consumers. The Fund's need for social accounting information is spelled out in the prospectus:

> The Fund is attempting to develop methods, based on available public information, by which it can rate the comparative effectiveness of companies in these matters.
>
> Such information is obtained from available reports and other documents filed with the Securities and Exchange Commission, from direct inquiry to companies which otherwise meet the Fund's investment criteria, and from selected newspapers and other publications.[15]

First Spectrum Fund's investment adviser, Spectrum Directors, Inc., has offered its social performance evaluations to other institutional investors (for a

---

14 *The Dreyfus Third Century Fund, Inc. Prospectus,* June 20, 1972.
15 *First Spectrum Fund, Inc. Prospectus,* December 22, 1972.

fee, of course, ranging downward from $500 annually for large institutions). Its "spectrographs" rate industries and firms in several categories of social performance. For example, the automobile industry is rated in seven categories: environment; fair employment; consumerism; financial matters (including development of a corporate social audit); foreign investment; military sales; and a variety of public policy issues including charitable contributions, minority recruitment, disclosure of information on corporate responsibility issues, and political contributions. Unfortunately the final, overall rating is simply a mean of the seven scores; thus all categories are weighted equally, and the final rating is heavily dependent on the initial selection of relevant categories.

Why should investors and shareholders impose social performance criteria on the companies in which they hold shares? Some of course are motivated by purely moral concerns. But there seems to be a growing tendency to consider social performance even when investment objectives are strictly economic. The response of a partner in a major San Francisco investment firm to a negative evaluation of American Electric Power Company (its environmental record was the worst of 15 electric utilities studied by The Council on Economic Priorities, a public interest research group) was to immediately sell all the American Electric Power stock in his discretionary accounts. He then called 70 or 80% of his nondiscretionary accounts and advised them that "any management that has allowed itself to get into such a bad condition on environmental issues must be poorly managed and therefore a poor investment."[16] Or as the senior vice-president for finance of Travelers Insurance Company (with over $1 billion invested in common stocks) recently observed: "If a company has a 'public be damned' attitude in this day and age, one could infer that the management is not too sharp."[17]

Social accounting and reporting are needed by present and potential investors, by large institutions and individuals. Some investors are powerful enough to command the information desired, but even they cannot ensure accuracy and honesty in the reports they receive. To protect both large and small investors, the Securities and Exchange Commission requires the periodic filing of a multitude of audited reports. Recently the SEC recognized the environmental dimensions of corporate performance by requiring companies to disclose the fi-

---

16 Described by Alice Tepper Marlin of The Council on Economic Priorities in the California CPA Foundation's Symposium on Measurement of Corporate Social Performance, Monterey, April 1973.
17 *Business Week,* January 19, 1974, p. 67.

nancial effects of compliance with environmental-protection laws. Disclosure must reflect any material impact on capital expenditures, earnings, and the company's competitive position. And if management has a reasonable basis for believing that *future* environmental compliance will have a significant financial impact, this too must be disclosed. Also any pending legal or administrative enforcement proceedings arising under environmental laws or regulations, or any known to be contemplated by governmental authorities, must be disclosed.[18]

Other government agencies also require reports containing social accounting information. These include the Environmental Protection Agency, the Equal Employment Opportunity Commission, and reports that must be posted under the Occupational Safety and Health Act. Such reports may not presently be available to the general public, but that their preparation is required means that management has already gone a long way in developing social accounting information. This information is available now for management's use and could be publicly reported at no additional preparation expense.

Many organized public interest groups seek corporate social performance information, and some have become adept at obtaining it without the company's cooperation. The Council on Economic Priorities reports illustrate how much information an outside group can put together, especially with the occasional sub rosa help of company employees; CEP reports include

- *Efficiency in Death: Manufacturers of Anti-Personnel Weapons*
- *Guide to Corporations: Where They Stand*
- *Paper Profits: Pollution in the Paper and Pulp Industry*
- *The Price of Power: Electric Utilities and the Environment*
- *Environmental Steel: Pollution in the Iron and Steel Industry*

Similar reports include Stephen Nowlan and Diana Russell Shayon's *Profiles of Involvement,* which catalogs 535 social action projects of 186 of the nation's largest corporations, and *Citibank,* Ralph Nader's Study Group Report on First National City Bank. A more dramatic form of reporting is used by Public

---

18 *Wall Street Journal,* April 24, 1973; and Securities and Exchange Commission Release No. 5235 under the Securities Act of 1933. In October 1975 the Commission proposed new rules that would require disclosure of material estimates of capital outlays for environmental control facilities, as well as disclosure of limited information about the extent to which a company has failed to meet any applicable environmental standards established pursuant to any federal statute.

Communication, Inc., which takes out advertisements naming companies and their products. A recent PCI ad on the back cover of *The New Republic* (April 13, 1974) listed the "10 Most Dangerous Car Recalls" by company name and model, and cited the defects for which the named cars had been recalled.

In these cases we see external groups accounting for corporate social performance and reporting their results and interpretations. One wonders whether the corporations studied wouldn't have been better off to do their own social accounting and reporting. At least they would have learned about the problems in time to prepare defenses or to institute changes, instead of being surprised with their dirty linen spread over the front page of the Sunday newspaper.

RESPONSES TO THE DEMAND

The major responses to demands for social performance information have, appropriately, come from corporations; these responses are considered in some detail in Chapter 2. But there have also been institutional responses.

The American Institute of Certified Public Accountants sponsored a round-table discussion on social accounting in April, 1972, with participants reflecting the views of sociologists, businessmen, political scientists, government officials, economists, and CPAs.[19] Other symposia, conferences, sessions, and seminars have been sponsored by the Battele Institute, the American Accounting Association, the Institute of Management Science, and the California Certified Public Accountants Foundation. The AICPA also appointed a Committee on Ecology in 1970 and, subsequently, a Committee on Social Measurement.

The AICPA's interest is further manifested in the inclusion of a social accounting problem in the theory section of the November 1973 CPA Examination. The second part of this problem is as follows:

Elmo's Davis Plant causes approximately as much pollution as Bland. Davis, however, is located in another state, where there is little likelihood of governmental regulation, and Elmo has no plans for pollution control at this plant. One of Elmo's officers, Mr. Pearce, says that uncontrolled pollution at Davis constitutes a very real cost to society, which is not recorded anywhere under current practice. He suggests that this "social cost" of the Davis Plant be included annually in Elmo's income statement. Further, he suggests that

---

19 *Social Measurement*, AICPA, 1972.

measurement of this cost is easily obtainable by reference to the depreciation on Bland's pollution control equipment.

Required:

1. Is Mr. Pearce necessarily correct in stating that costs associated with Davis' pollution are entirely unrecorded? Explain.

2. Evaluate Mr. Pearce's proposed method of measuring the annual "social cost" of Davis' pollution.

3. Discuss the merit of Mr. Pearce's suggestion that a "social cost" be recognized by a business enterprise.[20]

The May 1974 CPA Examination also included a problem involving pollution control equipment.

Even more significant is the report of the Study Group on the Objectives of Financial Statements (the "Trueblood Committee"). This distinguished group, appointed by the AICPA, represented the first major effort of the accounting profession to define the objectives of corporate financial reports. The concluding objective of the twelve proposed by the study group is

An objective of financial statements is to report on those activities of the enterprise affecting society which can be determined and described or measured and which are important to the role of the enterprise in its social environment.[21]

Several committees of the American Accounting Association have been studying the need for possible approaches to social accounting. These committees, along with references to their reports, are as follows:

- Committee on Non-Financial Measures of Effectiveness (*The Accounting Review*, Supplement to Vol. XLVI, 1971, pp. 164–211).
- Committee on Measures of Effectiveness for Social Programs (*The Accounting Review*, Supplement to Vol. XLVII, 1972, pp. 336–396).
- Committee on Environmental Effects of Organization Behavior (*The Accounting Review*, Supplement to Vol. XLVIII, 1973, pp. 72–119).
- Committee on Measurement of Social Costs (*The Accounting Review*, Supplement to Vol. XLIX, 1974, pp. 98–113).

---

20 *Examination in Accounting Theory*, AICPA, November 9, 1973. Copyright 1973 by the AICPA, Inc. Used by permission.
21 *Objectives of Financial Statements*, AICPA, 1973.

In 1972 the National Association of Accountants established a Committee on Accounting for Corporate Social Performance. It recently issued its first report in two parts: a Statement of Objectives and Procedures, and a taxonomy on Areas of Corporate Social Performance. Because of its general interest, the Committee's report is reproduced in its entirety in the Appendix to this chapter. It appears that the NAA has made a long-term commitment to the development of corporate social accounting.

In contrast to these positive responses to the demand for social accounting, and especially in opposition to the conclusion of the Study Group on the Objectives of Financial Statements, the Financial Analysts Federation has taken the position that social cost reporting is outside the proper scope of financial reporting, although perhaps social costs "should be footnoted as a matter of general interest."[22] Similarly, a Financial Executives Research Foundation study found that a narrow majority of the interviewed companies favored disclosure of expenditures for environmental programs such as pollution control and abatement (but not in terms of earnings per share); the study found that management was nearly unanimous in the view that reporting on other social issues, such as minority employment practices and product safety, should be optional.[23]

CONCLUSION

The demand for social accounting information appears to be substantial and growing. Various segments of the corporation's public—investors, customers, government bodies, public interest groups, professional organizations—are imposing social performance standards on the corporation and seeking information to judge the performance. If the corporation doesn't provide the information willingly, public interest groups may ferret it out anyway or the government may require it.

Large institutional investors are moving not only to base investment decisions partially on social performance criteria but also to vote their vast shareholdings in favor of proxy proposals dealing with social issues. Indeed, some are even initiating such proposals. Churches, universities, foundations,

---

22 Reported in *The Businessman's View of the Purposes of Financial Reporting,* Financial Executives Research Foundation, 1973, p. 49.
23 *Ibid.,* pp. 35–37.

and more recently banks, insurance companies, and mutual funds possess tremendous leverage to pry loose social accounting data, and they are starting to use that leverage.

But for many corporations the most significant demand is internal. Directors, management, and employees are calling for relevant social information in many cases, and most of the social accounting discussed in the next chapter was instigated in response to internal, not external, forces.

Of course not all corporations have faced these demands. Some are in industries that cause few social problems and are not much in the public eye; others are small enough to have so far avoided the pressures of their larger competitors. And some simply aren't listening.

Perhaps a corporation can ignore the demands for social accounting. Perhaps this is a fad that will soon pass. If it does, the skeptical firm will have avoided some cost; but if it doesn't go away, that firm may incur substantially greater costs—in public embarrassment, lost goodwill, disappointed employees, "catch-up" costs, and lawsuits.

Appendix
Report of the National Association of Accountants Committee on Accounting for Corporate Social Performance

STATEMENT OF OBJECTIVES AND PROCEDURES

I. Scope

Corporate activities have social as well as economic impacts. Accounting for corporate performance requires systematic measurements. Measurement is the process of evaluating objects or events according to rules consistently applied. In accounting for social performance, monetary units do not necessarily apply to its entire scope and may need to be complemented by other forms of measurement. It is the stated objective of the committee to develop systems of accounting for corporate social performance.

Management Accounting, February 1974, pp. 39–41. Copyright 1974 by NAA. Reprinted by permission.

II. Purposes

A. Internal
  1. Improve the decision-making process by:
    a. Assisting in the process of establishing goals, objectives and priorities in planning the use of monetary, physical and human resources.
    b. Educating and motivating managers to think through the social consequences of all decisions.
  2. Provide a basis for the continuing internal appraisal of social performance.
B. External
  1. Ultimately to provide consistent bases and reasonable uniformity for companies to measure social performance and to report to the public.
  2. Ultimately to provide a basis for independent attestation of corporate reports on social performance.

III. Procedure

A. Identify and classify areas of corporate social impact which may be measured. These will require additions and deletions as social values change.
B. Develop objective systems of measurement which may be used in assessing corporate social impact. Such systems may be numeric, in monetary or in non-monetary terms; or descriptive.
C. Through empirical research, test the categories of social impact and the feasibility and practicality of various measurement systems.
D. Revise and refine the categories of social impact and systems of measurement as indicated by the empirical research.
E. Maintain liaison with other professional and public bodies interested in the subject.

IV. Communication

A. Report in *Management Accounting* on committee progress at least semi-annually.
B. Publish drafts at each step of the procedure.

C. Issue NAA statements recommending methods of measuring corporate social performance; initially for internal purposes and ultimately for public reporting.

AREAS OF CORPORATE SOCIAL PERFORMANCE

I. Introduction

Corporate activities have social as well as economic impacts. For example, economic activities are measured by financial accounting procedures and are reported in financial statements. There are established standards for this. There are, however, no established standards for measuring and reporting corporate social performance.

Social performance reflects the impact of a corporation's activities upon society. This embodies the performance of its economic functions and other actions taken to contribute to the quality of life. These activities may extend beyond meeting the letter of the law, the pressures of competition or the requirements of contracts.

II. Relevance of Profitability to Corporate Social Performance

While categories of social performance of corporations include social efforts and impacts that are not captured by the economic and financial assessments of conventional accounting, the social relevance of conventional accounting measures must not be overlooked. The social significance of a corporation's net income should be recognized and then supplemented by measures of additional social effort and impact to determine a more nearly total measure of corporate performance. Thus it is appropriate to consider the social significance of net income before dealing with the more obvious social performance categories.

In this respect, profits are fundamental. Perpetuation of a private sector corporation and its potential for continued social contributions depends upon a satisfactory degree of profitability. Thus, net income is basically a short-run assessment of wealth creation which has social significance. Resources provided by this net income may be variously distributed thus providing various amounts of social product, but a profitable organization necessarily provides satisfaction for its many constituencies.

While relationships between economic and social phenomena are complicated, they are in many aspects complementary, and it would be a serious mistake to assume otherwise. Until these relationships are understood better it appears reasonable to pursue the subject of corporate social performance measurement by dealing with an expanded set of performance categories that build onto the present economic-based measures familiar to accountants and business managers.

III. Recognizing Corporate Social Performance

Social performance of corporations is of increasing concern to management, investors and the general public, but this performance is not measured and reported in a systematic manner. An important prerequisite for the orderly measuring and reporting of social performance is the proper identification of areas of social activity.

Areas of social performance need to be identified in order to assist management: (*1*) in establishing goals, objectives and priorities; (*2*) in planning the use of monetary, physical and human resources; and (*3*) in measuring progress. Because social performance has economic impacts, consideration of corporate social activities demands consideration of the economic consequences of each.

Further, social performance which is beneficial in one area may be somewhat adverse in another. Again, areas need to be identified so the necessity for trade-offs can be given consideration in management decisions. An example would be a decision to close a plant for which an air pollution problem cannot be solved without incurring significant costs versus making the required expenditures at the location in order to continue to provide employment continuity.

Also, identification is necessary as the first step in public reporting. *The Report of the Study Group on the Objectives of Financial Statements—* American Institute of Certified Public Accountants states:

"An objective of financial statements is to report on those activities of the enterprise affecting society which can be determined and described or measured and which are important to the role of the enterprise in its social environment."

Such reports should meet the qualitative characteristics of reporting stated by this study group (Chapter 10) namely relevance and materiality, reliability, freedom from bias, comparability, consistency and understandability.

IV. Major Areas of Social Performance

Social performance may be considered under the following four major areas (in alphabetical order):

A. Community involvement
B. Human resources
C. Physical resources and environmental contributions
D. Product or service contributions

Community involvement includes those socially oriented activities which tend primarily to benefit the general public. "Community" in this sense denotes more than the specific geographic area in which the corporation has plants and offices.

Human resources is an internal area. It covers that social performance which is directed to the well-being of employees.

Physical resources and environmental contributions include those activities which are directed toward alleviating or preventing environmental deterioration. Again, these relate to more than the geographical location of corporate facilities. An example would be a product which is inherently polluting and thus would have adverse environmental effects wheresoever it was used.

Product or service contributions of a social nature deal with relations with customers, or effects on society accruing or arising from products or services. They reflect the concerns of a corporation for generating and maintaining customer satisfaction over and above that of a *caveat emptor* attitude.

These four major areas of social performance are neither exhaustive nor mutually exclusive. For example, a decision as to a plant location would certainly give consideration to community involvement, environmental contributions and human resources. They are intended to encourage uniformity in appraising social performance.

The following list of items under each of the four major areas identifies typical examples of social performance. The lists are not intended to be all inclusive. Neither are the items listed in any sequence of importance. Comments following each item are for explanation.

A. COMMUNITY INVOLVEMENT

1. General philanthropy—Corporate support of educational institutions, cultural activities, recreational programs, health and community welfare agencies and similar eleemosynary organizations

2. Public and private transportation—Alleviating or preventing urban transportation problems, including the provision of mass transportation of employees
3. Health services—Providing health care facilities and services and the support of programs to reduce disease and illness
4. Housing—Improving the standard of dwellings, the construction of needed dwellings and the financing of housing renovation and construction
5. Aid in personal and business problems—Alleviation of problems related to the physically handicapped, child care, minority businesses, disadvantaged persons, etc.
6. Community planning and improvement—Programs of urban planning and renewal, crime prevention, etc.
7. Volunteer activities—Encouraging and providing time for employees to be active as volunteers in community activities
8. Specialized food programs—The provision of meals to meet the dietary needs of the aged, the infirm, the disadvantaged child and other groups
9. Education—The development and implementation of educational programs to supplement those of the public or private schools such as work study programs; and employee service on school boards, school authorities and college university trustee and advisory boards

B. HUMAN RESOURCES

1. Employment practices—Providing equal job opportunities for all persons, creation of summer job opportunities for students, and recruiting in depressed areas
2. Training programs—Providing programs for all employees to increase their skills, earning potential and job satisfaction
3. Promotion policies—Recognizing the abilities of all employees and providing equal opportunities for promotion
4. Employment continuity—Scheduling production so as to minimize lay-offs and recalls, maintaining facilities in efficient operating condition so that they will not have to be abandoned because of deterioration, and exploring all feasible alternatives to closing a facility
5. Remuneration—Maintaining a level of total salaries and wages plus benefits which is in line with others in either the industry or community
6. Working conditions—Providing safe, healthful and pleasant working environment

7. Drugs and alcohol— Providing education and counseling for employees to prevent or alleviate problems in these and similar areas
8. Job enrichment—Providing the most meaningful work experiences practical for all employees
9. Communications—Establishing and maintaining two-way communication between all levels of employees to secure suggestions, to provide information as to what the company is actually doing and how each department's activities relate to the total corporate activity, and to inform employees' families and friends of corporate activities

C. PHYSICAL RESOURCES AND ENVIRONMENTAL CONTRIBUTIONS

1. Air—Timely meeting of the law and going beyond the law in avoiding the creation of, alleviating, or eliminating pollutants in these areas
2. Water—Timely meeting of the law and going beyond the law in avoiding the creation of, alleviating, or eliminating pollutants in these areas
3. Sound—Timely meeting of the law and going beyond the law in avoiding the creation of, alleviating, or eliminating pollutants in these areas
4. Solid waste—Disposal of solid waste in such a manner as to minimize contamination, reduce its bulk, etc., and the design of processes and products which will minimize the creation of solid waste
5. Use of scarce resources—The conservation of existing energy sources, the development of new energy sources, and the conservation of scarce materials
6. Aesthetics—The design and location of facilities in conformance with surroundings and with pleasing architecture and landscaping

D. PRODUCT OR SERVICE CONTRIBUTIONS

1. Completeness and clarity of labeling, packaging, and marketing representation—Assurance that labeling and representation as to methods of use, limitations on use, hazards of use, shelf-life, quantity of contents, and quality *cannot be misunderstood*
2. Warranty provisions—Adherence to all stated or implied warranties of a product with implementation through timely recalls, repairs or replacements
3. Responsiveness to consumer complaints—Prompt and complete responses to all complaints received

4. Consumer education—Literature and media programs to keep consumers informed of product or service characteristics, methods and areas of use of products, and of planned product changes or discontinuances

5. Product quality—Assurance through adequate control—"quality assurance"—that quality is at least equal to what customers may reasonably expect on the basis of company representations

6. Product safety—Design or formulation and packaging of products to minimize possibilities of harm or injury in product use

7. Content and frequency of advertising—Giving full consideration to the omission of any media material which may be adverse or offensive; and the avoidance of repetition to the extent that it becomes repugnant

8. Constructive research—Orienting technical and market research to meet defined social needs and to avoid creating social and environmental problems or to minimize such problems; e.g., energy consumption □

Lord, Lord, how this world is given to lying!
Shakespeare, King Henry IV

2 Corporate Social Accounting: The State of the Art

This chapter examines the current state of corporate social accounting and presents several illustrative cases. Both internal social accounting, which is not publicly reported, and external social reporting are explored.

Although some include human resource accounting within the definition of social accounting, the developing consensus appears to be that human resource accounting is merely a modification of traditional financial accounting to capitalize as assets costs that have heretofore been expensed. Thus human resource accounting is not included here within the scope of social accounting.[1]

INTERNAL SOCIAL ACCOUNTING

Corporations are naturally going to experiment with social accounting before publicly disclosing any results; disclosure is only the tip of the iceberg. But how extensive is such experimentation? How many corporations have applied or are presently applying social accounting internally?

A 1973 survey of corporations undertaken by John Corson and George Steiner for the Committee for Economic Development[2] provides some tentative answers. This survey obtained a good representation from different-size groups and different industries, and should thus be fairly representative of U.S. corporations.

---

1 Readers interested in this subject may want to consult Eric Flamholtz' *Human Resource Accounting* (Dickenson Publishing Co., 1974).

2 John J. Corson and George A. Steiner, *Measuring Business's Social Performance: The Corporate Social Audit* (Committee for Economic Development, 1974).

The key question asked in the survey was whether the responding companies had attempted, within the period since January 1, 1972, to inventory or assess what had been done in any of several socially oriented activity fields listed. *Seventy-six percent answered yes!* Note that these responses do not necessarily reflect the extent of social involvement or responsibility, but rather efforts to "inventory or assess" the company's activities in such areas—in other words, some degree of social accounting. Unfortunately the meaning of this result is not altogether clear because the researchers included—along with assistance to education, recruitment of the disadvantaged, ensuring employment and advancement opportunities for minorities, pollution abatement, and other activities normally listed as social programs—several activities that some would interpret as falling within the traditional economic role of the firm, such as "increasing productivity in the private sector of the economy," and "improving the innovativeness and performance of business management."

A similar study conducted by the Gallagher Report, Inc.,[3] obtained what at first appear to be significantly different results. In response to the question, "Does your company give itself an annual social audit?" only 14% responded affirmatively (although 21% of those responding negatively indicated they were considering such an audit). This apparent difference between the Corson and Steiner study and the Gallagher study is probably due to Gallagher's use of the more definite and formal term *social audit* (many companies engaged in some modest form of social accounting would be unwilling to label the effort a social audit) as well as the exclusion of occasional or one-time efforts by the reference to an annual social audit.

What motivates corporate management to initiate some form of social accounting? The Corson and Steiner study also sheds light on this subject. Respondents were asked, "If your company has made any type of social audit (i.e., an inventory and/or assessment), what purpose (or purposes) led management to undertake it?" The four leading responses, accounting for 56% of all purposes indicated, were the following:

1. To examine what the company is actually doing in selected areas.
2. To appraise or evaluate performance in selected areas.
3. To identify those social programs which the company feels it ought to be pursuing.
4. To inject into the general thinking of managers a social point of view.

---

3 Reported in *Financial Executive*, March 1973, p. 8.

Social accounting (or a "social audit") may take various forms, ranging from simple and inexpensive to complex and costly. This range is illustrated in the following representative approaches:

1. Informal reviews of social responsibility activities at periodic meetings of branch or district managers.
2. An "inventory" of social actions.
3. Cost estimates of social programs and activities.
4. Some sort of "impact analysis" of social programs, as well as an attempt to estimate the effects of socially undesirable actions (such as air pollution).
5. A comprehensive evaluation of the social impact of the company.
6. Public disclosure of any of the above results.

These and other approaches have been followed by corporations in their efforts to respond to the rising demand for social accounting. Any prescribed approach will of course be modified to reflect the circumstances and problems of a particular corporation. To provide something of the flavor of the difficulties encountered and results obtained, the internal social accounting efforts of two companies are described in detail.

TRW, Inc.

The TRW effort has been described by a company executive as an "audit on the back of an envelope." A review of TRW's approach and the problems encountered should be informative to anyone considering a similarly modest approach.

TRW is a highly divisionalized "conglomerate" with a great deal of divisional autonomy. Its move toward a social audit began with a survey of shareholders to determine their reactions to company involvement in social issues. The results were unexpectedly positive. TRW then established the office of Vice President for Community Affairs, having the initial responsibility of studying TRW's role and approach to the social responsibility area. This led to a decision, in September 1972, to undertake some sort of internal social audit of TRW. This effort produced an internal report having the following sections:

I. Minorities
   A. Employment, Training, and Promotion
   B. Minority Enterprise
   C. Overseas Investment (South Africa)

II. Pollution Control
    A. Progress to Date
    B. Problems
III. Relevant Product Lines
    A. Community Systems
    B. Consumer-Related Products and Services
    C. Defense Contracts
IV. Contributions
    A. Dollars
    B. Personal Involvement
V. Communications (re corporate social responsibility)
    A. External
    B. Internal

Each subtopic contains a narrative ranging from two sentences to one page. A few dollar costs and percentages are given, with several references to specific cases or examples.

A fairly informal approach was used to gather the information. The information regarding minority employment, training, and promotion had already been gathered by the personnel staff for the Equal Employment Opportunity Commission's report. Three brief examples of TRW's support of minority enterprise were cited, and it was further noted that the company, as a government contractor, was required to follow certain practices in the selection of its suppliers. The extent of investment in South Africa was taken from previous news releases (which had announced a reduction in South Africa investments for profitability, not social, reasons).

The company had performed a study of pollution control in 1970, and this was simply updated. The information on the social impact of product lines was taken almost entirely from previous output of the public relations department. As this was being pulled together for the report, it began to appear that there was an increasing level of product liability claims. This was surprising to the company and was considered to be a significant revelation of the social audit.

The company's relative standing in defense business was taken from a published report of the Council on Economic Priorities, a public-interest research group. Information on contributions came from the manager of the company's foundations, and the report on communications was developed largely from the public relations people.

As might be expected for such a first effort at this stage in the development of social accounting, the TRW internal social evaluation is spotty and irregular. The selection of areas to be studied reflects only one set out of many possible choices; others might emphasize health and safety (this area was added for TRW's "second round," energy consumption and conservation, or solid waste control. (This is not so much a criticism as an observation about the present lack of standards for social accounting.) Most important, however, the report is weak in the identification of problems—it is not "attention-directing." Thus it might be read with interest but is unlikely to generate action directed toward solving present problems or preventing future ones. According to a company official, however, the report did achieve the primary objective of demonstrating to the company president that the "audit" was a tool that could be useful in eliminating problems within the company.

TRW next entered what they considered to be the "second round" in this effort, which was renamed the "corporate responsibility inventory." Divisions were asked to provide greater in-depth information by the use of a 19-page questionnaire. Greater resistance was encountered in obtaining the desired information than previously because of the more intensive probing and the possible deficiencies that might be illustrated.

The second round effort was confined to the United States. The company planned to enter the third round in 1974 and explore the social impact of foreign activities. Systematic quantification, beyond simply adding up selected costs here and there, was not contemplated until 1975 or later.

What is the use of all this effort? It appears that eventually TRW's social accounting will identify deficiencies in company performance and departures from company policy in the social responsibility area. Some pleasant surprises might also occur, as when it was discovered that one division had already set minority enterprise purchasing goals and had doubled these in 1973. The company is now in a much better position to respond to inquiries about its social efforts from shareholders, government agencies, public-interest groups, and the press. And, although this can only be speculated, an increased moral and social concern may be developing throughout the organization, from top to bottom.

Bank of America

Bank of America was the target of several violent demonstrations toward the end of the 1960s. In evident response to these attacks and the developing corporate social responsibility movement, an ad hoc, high-level group began to meet in an attempt to develop some social priorities for the bank. The initial priorities were minority housing, the environment, and social unrest.

This resulted in a program of inventorying the bank's activities in these special areas. The inventory is updated two or three times a year, and the resulting report is distributed to employees.

The bank next put together a fairly rough estimate of the costs of these activities; this was completed in 1971. About the same time the president of Bank of America made a speech urging a national as well as a corporate system of social indicators. This seems to have had the effect of ensuring the bank's commitment to social accounting.

Paralleling TRW's Vice President for Community Affairs, the office of Executive Vice President for Social Policy was established by Bank of America in 1972. Since this executive has the responsibility of seeing that all aspects of the bank's performance meet social responsibility criteria, the social responsibility area at Bank of America was integrated with the main functions of the business. But unlike the main functions, no reporting system existed for the social responsibility area.

An effort to gather social responsibility information resulted in a 49-page "Social Policy Report 1972." The bulk of this report is devoted to a cost-benefit analysis of special (i.e., not "mainstream") programs. Direct costs, allocated costs, and sacrificed income were used to obtain cost estimates; salary costs were included only for people working *full-time* in social programs. Only dollar benefits (e.g., interest income, government reimbursement) were recognized; it was felt that measurement of the impact on society of these programs was impossible at that time. (An effort was made, however, to determine the degree to which the *objectives* of special social programs were being met; this involved the use of mailed questionnaires and personal interviews with borrowers.) Finally, the opportunity cost approach was applied by deducting the estimated yields from alternative uses of the same funds, to arrive at the net cost to the bank.

Internal social accounting at Bank of America is obviously well advanced, with its comprehensiveness, cost data, and use of opportunity costs. In fact, internal social accounting in general can be expected to evolve more rapidly than external social reporting because, with all its risks, the internal effort is not likely to be subjected to the scrutiny of a critical and sometimes disbelieving society.

Nevertheless, a considerable amount of external social reporting is occurring, and it is to this aspect of social accounting that we now turn our attention.

EXTERNAL SOCIAL REPORTING

Most social reporting occurs in the annual report. An unpublished study by Associate Dean Irwin Jarett, of the Southern Illinois University Medical School, showed that 45% of the responding companies used the annual report for disclosure of information on corporate social responsibility. The Corson and Steiner study discussed at the beginning of this chapter also found that the annual report was used by 45% of the respondents to disclose results of their social activity inventories or assessments.

Ernst & Ernst has studied social measurement disclosures in the annual reports of *Fortune* 500 companies for several years. They found that the number of companies making such disclosures has increased in each of the last two years:[4]

	1973	1972	1971
Companies reporting social measurement disclosures	298	286	239
Companies with no social measurement disclosures	198	206	226
Reports not readily available	4	8	35
	500	500	500

The percentage of companies making such disclosures increased from 51% in 1971 to 58% in 1972, with a nominal increase to 60% in 1973.

A *Business Week* analysis of annual reports of 100 companies over several years shows the following pattern of disclosure of "concern for corporate responsibilities":[5]

1970	30%
1971	60
1972	64
1973	22
1974	35

---

4 "A Special Study of Social Measurement Disclosures in Annual Reports," Ernst & Ernst, undated monograph.
5 "An Open Door Policy for Annual Reports," *Business Week,* May 12, 1975, p. 48.

The *Business week* results for recent years appear to be inconsistent with those of Ernst & Ernst. This may reflect *Business Week's* smaller sample, or it may reflect different definitions of "social measurement" disclosures and "concern for corporate responsibilities" disclosures.

A study by Sidney Jones of annual reports issued by 55 of the larger companies in the *Fortune* 500 is consistent with *Business Week's* results.[6] Jones' study, which covered the period 1960 to 1970, found that roughly 25% of the 1970 reports contained a special section devoted to corporate social responsibilities. It is informative to note the matters discussed in these sections; the topics and the number of times they were referenced in the 55 annual reports are as follows:

Subject	Number of References	
	1970	1960
Air pollution control	39	0
Water pollution control	31	0
Employee—disadvantaged worker hiring	21	0
Visual pollution control	19	0
Safety	19	10
Community involvement—civic	16	5
Support of education and noncompany basic research	15	15
Employee—external education and training	10	12
Community involvement—urban development	9	1
Charities	8	3
Corporate organization for social responsibility	7	0

Areas of corporate social concern change over time, and this is reflected in social reporting. The Jones tabulation, for example, shows that the dominate concerns in 1960 were support of education, employee education, and safety; by 1970 the emphasis had shifted to pollution control and hiring of the disadvantaged (although concern in almost all areas was up). Indeed, the 1970 annual reports of some 70% of the larger companies in the United States dis-

6 Sidney L. Jones, "Reporting Corporate Social Responsibility Activities," paper presented at the Financial Management Association National Conference, October 8, 1971.

cussed pollution control; this proportion increases to 80% for companies in heavily polluting industries.[7]

Given the temper of the times, we might expect less attention to social awareness expenditures outside the area of pollution control. Nevertheless, one sixth of the companies included in the AICPA's study of 1972 annual reports disclosed expenditures in these other areas.[8]

These studies show that many companies are reporting *something* about their social activities and concerns, using the annual report as the primary reporting vehicle. Several examples of such reporting are now discussed to illustrate the variety of approaches found in current practice. These range from purely narrative descriptions of social responsibility activities to a fully quantified "social audit" report.

The Quaker Oats Company

The simplest form of presentation is illustrated by the 1974 annual report of The Quaker Oats Company. It devotes a few paragraphs to the topics of people and public responsibility. No dollar amounts are reported nor are any standards or norms indicated. The report is thus not strong on social reporting, but it does represent a rudimentary approach.

International Business Machines Corporation

In addition to a narrative description of actions and policies, a company may disclose some quantitative indications of the extent of its social responsibility activities. This approach is illustrated in a section on "IBM and Society" in IBM's 1972 annual report, which disclosed, for example, that

- 25 IBM professionals were on loan for a year at full pay to 25 colleges with large enrollments of disadvantaged students;
- during 1972, over a hundred IBM employees were on social service leaves working on problems ranging from fighting drug abuse on city streets to promoting light industry at an Indian reservation;
- over 200 projects have been supported through IBM's Fund for Community Service;

---

7 Doyle Z. Williams, James C. Caldwell, and Belverd E. Needles, "Reporting Pollution Control Costs in Annual Reports," unpublished paper, Texas Tech University, 1972.

8 *Accounting Trends & Techniques 1973,* AICPA, 1973, p. 241.

- over 700 managers were from minority groups;
- during the preceding year, the number of women managers in IBM increased by almost a third, bringing the United States total to more than 600.

The section also discusses, without mention of any quantities, other support provided to minority education and minority-owned enterprises, a study of the need for privacy and security of computer information, and pollution control efforts.

While social reporting with some sort of quantification may provide more information than a strictly narrative report, it is obvious from such reports as IBM's that selection of quantities to be disclosed is at the discretion of management. The disclosure is thus unlikely to satisfy the reader's desire for information and is likely to be inconsistent from one year to the next and from one company to another. Furthermore, raw quantities without standards for evaluation are of little use to the reader who is not knowledgeable about the reporting firm and its industry.

The Chase Manhattan Corporation

On another step up the social reporting ladder, a corporation could report both quantities and relevant dollar amounts. This approach is illustrated by a section of Chase Manhattan's 1972 annual report entitled "Social Responsibility." The report notes that an additional $90 million was allocated to the financing of low- and moderate-income housing and related community facilities such as day-care centers, and that this resulted in more than 2200 units of new housing, nearly 750 mortgages in inner-city areas, and day-care facilities for over 200 children; loans of some $19 million were made to nearly 300 businesses that did not meet conventional credit standards but had high potential; purchases from minority businesses rose by 20% in 1972; and 415 staff members shared their time and expertise in nonprofit programs. Apparently, efforts are being made at Chase to spread the concern for social responsibility into the lower echelons, for the report notes that all departments were asked to include specific social responsibility goals in the formal planning process.

In some companies, social accounting ends with the disclosure of a few random pieces of information in the annual report. This is evidently not the case at Chase Manhattan (or at Bank of America, as discussed earlier in this chapter). The Chase Manhattan report notes:

> . . . we established a task force to explore better means of measuring the costs and benefits of our programs. The final integration of social and economic concerns will demand more sophisticated and accurate ways to quantify and evaluate long-term implications. The task force suggested a number of actions that are now being followed. These include a pilot cost-benefits format, a unified accounting system, and the establishment of an action research project to measure indirect social and economic benefits in a selected neighborhood.[9]

Eastern Gas and Fuel Associates

Raw data are meaningless; we must have some basis for comparison. This basis might, as a minimum, be the prior year's performance of the reported entity, or it might be an industry average. Other alternatives include targets or standards set by the reporting entity, or norms established by government agencies or professional bodies. At present very little of the social information reported by corporations is related to norms or standards.

Eastern Gas and Fuel Associates' social reporting is a significant exception. Special sections included with the 1972, 1973, and 1974 annual reports provide good *comparative* information in four areas: industrial safety, minority employment, charitable giving, and pensions. The 1974 report, reproduced in Exhibit 2-1, also states future goals for these areas of concern.

The accident frequency rate is expressed in terms of the number of lost time accidents per million employee hours (much more meaningful than the absolute number of accidents) for four years running. Accident severity rate is similarly presented as the number of employee days lost per million employee hours for the last four years. Fatalities are given in absolute numbers for four years, but the figures are so small that comparisons with employee hours worked might not be meaningful.

Minority employment is presented as a percentage of total company employment and also broken down by job classification. In previous years a divisional breakdown was given.

Charitable giving is presented and related to pretax income, dollars per em-

---

9 *The Chase Manhattan Corporation Annual Report 1972*, p. 22.

EXHIBIT 2-1   Of Social Concern

In 1974, Eastern Gas and Fuel Associates continued its effort of the past several years for improving both its performance and its measure of performance in several recognized areas of special social concern. This effort merely affirms our intention to conduct our business in a socially responsible manner.

In the beginning, Eastern saw itself as something of a pioneer in such efforts, reaching out ahead of requirements for awareness and levels of disclosure in matters of minority employment, industrial safety, corporate contributions and pension funding. But in social concerns, as in other matters, we face evermoving targets. Some contend that social responsibility has fallen victim to the troubled economic climate. From our experience, however, it seems that legislation has now leapfrogged formerly pioneering goals. While pioneering and rhetoric may have faded, the underlying interest and efforts are preserved, if not intensified. Actual accomplishments may, in fact, outstrip earlier goals.

In our own case, matters of social concern, formerly handled optionally and informally, are now an integral part of everyday business operations. The task now is not one of reminder, but of a built-in constant attempt to keep up with advancing social goals expressed in law and in custom. Concrete examples can be found in the strict new industrial health and safety standards, highly regulated recruiting and employment practices, and the recent complex new pension legislation. Within that kind of a general atmosphere our performance during 1974 is highlighted by the following statistics.

1. Industrial Safety

| | Accidents | | | | Fatalities | |
| | Frequency Rate | | Severity* Rate | | | |
	1973	1974	1973	1974	1973	1974
Coal and Coke	76	82	4822	2826	8	3
Gas	10	11	60	59	0	0
Marine	14	30	404	875	0	1
EFGA Average	39	51	2165	1622	8	4

*Excluding days charged for fatalities.

Our safety performance in 1974 was at best mixed. While there were improvements in measures of severity compared to 1973 we fell short of our goal of realizing a 10% improvement overall. The rather dramatic swing in coal which indicates more accidents of a less severe nature is in part due to more definitive reporting techniques.

EXHIBIT 2-1 *(Continued)*

2. Minority Employment

Minority Employment Levels

| | 1973 | | 1974 | |
	No.	% of Total	No.	% of Total
Officers and Managers	20	1.5	21	1.5
Professional and Technical	27	4.2	30	4.1
Clerical	70	8.1	84	8.2
Skilled	369	7.3	381	8.3
Unskilled	203	12.2	262	12.4
Total EGFA	689	7.3%	778	7.9%

Minority employment, both in terms of absolute numbers and percentage of total work force, showed substantial improvement both over 1973 and in relation to our stated overall 1974 goal of 7.5%. This was achieved despite new acquisitions in the gas division which reduced their percentage minority work force appreciably from 8.2% (1973) to 6.9% (1974). During the same period, coal rose from 7.0% to 7.5% and marine from 7.8% to 11.1%.

3. Charitable Giving

Total Charitable Giving

	1973	1974
Total Contributions	$289,999	$356,046
Per cent of pre-tax income	1.4%	0.6%
$ per employee equivalent	29.70	34.65
Earnings per share equivalent	1.6¢	2.6¢

Total contributions of $356,046 represent an increase of 21% over charitable giving in 1973 but fell below our goal of about 1% pre-tax income. The substantial increase in earnings per share equivalent is attributable to this increase as well as to a reduced average number of shares outstanding. The percentage of giving by category of interest in 1974 was at 40% for Health & Welfare, 19% for Higher Education, and 41% for Civic & Cultural, representing a shift toward Civic & Cultural causes.

EXHIBIT 2-1   (*Continued*)

4. **Pensions**

*Annual Cost of Pension
and Welfare Plans*

	(*$000*)	
	1973	*1974*
Union Welfare & Pension Plans	$ 7,519	$ 6,155
Other Formal and Informal Plans	4,040	5,773
	$11,559	$11,928

Additional funding costs in 1974, which in part reflect improved pension benefits and expanded employee coverage, were partially offset by lower contributions resulting from a decrease in coal production. Eastern has already moved energetically to comply with detailed requirements for reporting of plans for which it has some responsibility.

5. **Other Areas**

Environmental matters continue as a prime concern in all our operations; new requirements stretch their ability to comply. Our river operations work constantly to prevent spillage or environmental damage, our mines are all engaged in approved safety or environmental compliance programs, and our coke plant was recently commended for improvements and described as one of the best controlled coke plants in the country today.

Goals For 1975

In an atmosphere heavy with new and changing legislation, much of our effort will be spent to accomplish full compliance with laws and regulations. Beyond that, we intend to intensify our safety efforts and improve upon our overall 1974 records by 10%. In minority employment, we hope to raise our percentage above 8% and continue our upward trend in employment level. We anticipate that with our broadened activities charitable giving will rise above $400,000 in 1975.

Source: *Eastern Gas and Fuel Associates Annual Report 1974.* Used by permission.

ployee, and earnings per share. Charitable giving is also reported by major recipient category.

Company contributions to pension and welfare plans are reported, but are not related to other bases of comparison.

Disclosure of future goals in the social performance area is almost unique (First National Bank of Minneapolis may be the only other company publicly disclosing future objectives of this sort). Indeed, reporting of specific, quantified future goals may be the most informative part of social reporting; it certainly is the most courageous.

Development of social accounting at Eastern Gas and Fuel was similar in a number of respects to the effort at TRW, Inc., described earlier in this chapter.[10] The initial impetus seems to have come from a frustrating absence of information about company performance in areas of social concern. In the summer of 1971, an MBA student was assigned to undertake a kind of social audit, an effort stymied by the near autonomy of the operating companies and the resulting difficulty of obtaining necessary information. This was followed by a stronger commitment in 1972 to undertake another social accounting, with one of the purposes being to simply inform management of what was going on in the company in certain social areas (this objective corresponds with the results of the Corson and Steiner study cited at the beginning of this chapter).

Health and safety, minority employment, charitable giving, and pensions were selected for study. The Director of Health and Safety requested data by letter from each mine or facility. Statistics on minority employment were obtained from EEOC filings and personnel records. Charitable giving was handled by Eastern Associated Foundation, and the required information was available there. Information about pension plans was pulled together from the various subsidiaries and divisions (and revealed the surprising fact that Eastern participated in 25 different pension plans). In addition, some of the required figures had been obtained during the summer 1971 effort.

Results in these four areas were published in a special insert to the 1972 Annual Report. The insert also included a short questionnaire for shareholders. The results of this questionnaire (500 responses out of 8800 stockholders) suggested that the shareholders were impressed by the company's honesty and openness in voluntarily revealing disappointing results. Many shareholders apparently judged Eastern a progressive company because it was working toward social accounting. One responded:

> Congratulations! Despite my loss of $2000 on your stock, it is heartening to note your humanitarian approach to life.[11]

---

10 This discussion of the internal development of Eastern Gas and Fuel's social accounting effort is based largely on Harvard Business School cases *Eastern Gas & Fuel Social Audit* (A) through (D), prepared by Research Assistant Terry Cauthorn under the supervision of Professor Raymond A. Bauer.

11 *Eastern Gas and Fuel Social Audit (D)*, p. 3.

Another noted:

> I am impressed with the attitude of social responsibility that is implicit in this report. All companies should do the same. I am more likely to hang on to my stock as a result of this.[12]

Of course some respondents were negative to the whole idea of social responsibility and social accounting, including one who simply said, "Make money."

As to the overall desirability of social accounting, some 69% of the responding shareholders felt that the Eastern social accounting report should either be enlarged (13%) or continued in about the same manner (56%).[13] Following these results, the company president announced that managers will be evaluated on the basis of performance in the four areas studied, and that other areas such as pollution may be added in the future. As we have seen, the report was continued in 1973 and 1974, with additional disclosure of goals for the future.

First National Bank of Minneapolis

Another exceptional example of comparative quantitative information is contained in the 1974 annual report of First National Bank of Minneapolis (Exhibit 2-2). According to the bank, the Social-Environmental Audit serves the following two important functions:

1. It identifies, measures and reports to the corporation's major constituencies the social costs and the social benefits of doing business;
2. It furnishes corporate policy makers with social impact information which, in turn, can be used in corporate decision making and long-term planning.[14]

The 1974 Social-Environmental Audit was preceded by a report in 1972 giving *community* data on job opportunities, income, health, public safety, housing, education, citizen participation, environmental matters, transportation, and culture. This information formed the basis in 1973 for "Community Priority Ratings," reported along with data on the bank's performance in these areas.

---

12 *Ibid.*, p. 4.
13 *Ibid.*, p. 12.
14 *First National Bank of Minneapolis 1974 Annual Report*, p. 25.

EXHIBIT 2-2

1974 Internal Social-Environmental Audit

FIRST NATIONAL BANK OF MINNEAPOLIS

		1974 Performance Level	Net Percentage Performance Differential '73-'74 (2)	1974 Objectives (3)	1974 Social Performance Index (4)	1975 Objectives (5)
Housing 1 (1)	1. Number of residential mortgage loans originated in 1974 to families living in a.) Minneapolis b.) Suburbs & St. Paul	a.) 360 b.) 967	35% / 30	+ / +	↑ / ↓	a.) 360 b.) 967
	2. Dollar amount of residential mortgage loans originated in 1974 to families in a.) Minneapolis b.) Suburbs & St. Paul	a.) $ 8,861,000 b.) $29,324,000	25 / 20	+ / +	↑ / ↑	a.) $ 8,861,000 b.) $29,324,000
	3. Number of outstanding home improvement loans made to families living in a.) Minneapolis b.) Suburbs & St. Paul	a.) 357 b.) 744	15 / 10			a.) 655 b.) 676
	4. Ratio originated residential mortgage loans to bank's total resources	1:50	5			1:50
	5. Foundation contribution	$10,000	0	$10,920	.92	$10,000
Education 2	1. Number of classes taken by employees paid by bank a.) internal b.) external	363 164 199	5% / 4	+ + +	↓ ↑ ↓	—
	2. Number of employees in bank college gift matching program	48	3 / 2	+	↑	55
	3. Employee community Involvement man-hours per month	1,129	1	+	↑	1,241
	4. Foundation contribution to educational institutions	$51,750	0	$50,006	1.03	$55,000
Public Safety 3	1. Accidents on bank premises involving employees — 1974 (Does not include sports)	26	80% / 80 / 40			26
	2. Accidents involving non-employees	14	20 / 0			14
Income 4	1. Clerical employees — monthly income related to area-wide averages	1:1.01				1:1
	2. Clerical employees — composite productivity relation to base 1973	1:1.06				1:1.10
Job Opportunities 5	1. Percent officers, managers and professionals (EEO defined) a.) women b.) racial minority	a.) 19.8 b.) 3.5	80% / 60 / 40	+ +	↑ ↑	a.) 23.8 b.) 4.2
	2. Percent of job categories posted	77	20 / 0	75	1.03	77
Health 6	1. Estimated commitment to treatment of alcoholism a.) money b.) man-hours	a.) $5,460 b.) 222	50%	+ 50% +100%	.61 1.39	—
	2. Number of days missed due to health problems per capita a.) women b.) men	a.) 3.43 b.) 1.65	40 / 30	a.) 5.0 b.) 2.3	a.) 1.7 b.) 4.3	a.) 3.43 b.) 1.65
	3. Prepaid health services (HMO) as employee health option a.) services offered h) dollar c.) man-hours	a.) 0 b.) $1,000 c.) 141	20 / 10 / 0	+ +	↓ ↑	a.) 0 b.) $1,500 c.) 160
Transportation 7	1. Percent employees taking bus to work	61	50% / 40 / 30	50	1.22	65
	2. Percent employees who come to work in car pools	17	20	30	.56	20
	3. Percent employees who drive to work alone	19	10 / 0	15	.79	15
Participation 8	1. Man-hours per month spent by employees in community activity a.) on bank time b.) non-bank time	4,632 585 4,047	50% / 40 / 30	+ 380 +	↑ 1.54 ↑	5,095 643 4,451
	2. Percent employees donating to United Way	83	20	+	↑	85
	3. Percent employees voting Nov. '74	75	10 / 0			—

EXHIBIT 2-2 *(Continued)*

		1974 Performance Level	Net Percentage Performance Differential '73-'74 (2)	1974 Objectives (3)	1974 Social Performance Index (4)	1975 Objectives (5)
Environment 9 (1)	1. Percent office paper which is recycled	18		+	▲	18.5
	2. Energy consumed by bank					
	a.) steam	44,727,500		44,355,075	.99	44,727,500
	b.) electric (in kilowatt hours 1-1-74 to 12-31-74)	13,095,560		−15%	.91	13,095,560
	3. Loan commitments to firms dealing in anti-pollution equipment	$8,382,000				
	4. Community involvement commitment in man-hours per month	153				168
	5. Foundation contribution	$5,000		$6,037	.83	$5,000
Culture 10	1. Level of commercial line commitments to cultural institutions	$4,000,000				$4,000,000
	2. Community involvement — man-hours/month	333				370
	3. Foundation contribution	$115,200		$113,514	.99	$135,200
Human Relations	1. Number minority business loan applicants	56			▲	
	2. Percent approved installment loan applications					
	a.) women	82				83
	b.) men	83				83
	3. Level of minority business purchases	$46,530		$45,440	1.01	$49,000
	4. Community involvement — man-hours/month	803		+	▲	883
	5. Foundation contribution	$20,500		$18,250	1.12	$23,500
Community Investment (6)	1. Commitment to lend money to businesses					
	a.) Minneapolis	$284,936,000				$284,936,000
	b.) Suburbs and St. Paul	$296,127,000				$296,127,000
	2. Commitments to lend money to civic institutions at other than market terms					
	a.) number	8				
	b.) amount	$8,700,000				$8,700,000
	3. Dollar volume of commercial mortgage loans originated in					
	a.) Minneapolis	$1,143,000				
	b.) Suburbs and St. Paul	$3,902,000				
	4. Dollar volume commercial construction and land development loans					
	a.) Minneapolis	$ 4,685,000		+	▼	
	b.) Suburbs and St. Paul	$26,905,000		+	▼	
	5. Estimated dollar value of personal loans outstanding/total personal savings deposits	$239,602,000/ $233,568,000		+	▲	
	6. Total Foundation Contribution	$421,000		$420,000	1.0	$445,000
Consumer Protection and Services	1. New consumer services offered	8				8
	2. Diversity of perspective — percent of Board members without a primary background as a business executive	8		+	▼	
	3. Student loans originated in 1974 a.) number b.) dollar volume	a.) 1,192 b.) $1,877,000				a.) 1,192 b.) $1,877,000

(1) Numbered categories listed in order of community priority as determined from 1972 First Minneapolis community Social-Environmental Audit.

(2) Net Percentage Performance Differential computed by: (a) determining the percentage difference in 1974 against 1973 for each indicator, (b) adding the percentage increases or decreases, and (c) dividing the result by the number of indicators used in the category

to determine the net change. Only indicators appearing in both the 1973 and 1974 audit are considered.

(3) Many 1974 objectives were specified only as increase (+) or decrease (—) because the 1974 corporate planning process was not time coordinated with the audit process.

(4) Where a numerical 1974 objective was specified for an indicator, the 1974 achievement was measured against that objective. 1.00 or

more indicates the objective was met or exceeded. Less than 1.00 indicates the extent to which the objective was not met. If the 1974 objective indicated an increase (+), the 1974 performance is reflected by an ▲ if the objective was met or by an ▼ if it was not.

(5) Objectives are set as a part of the 1975 corporate management plan.

(6) Entitled Community Commitment in 1973.

Source: *First National Bank of Minneapolis. 1974 Annual Report.* Used by permission.

The First Minneapolis report indicates the relative importance to the community of each component, reports relevant physical and dollar amounts, provides for comparison with objectives for the present year, and indicates objectives for the following year. "A major objective for 1975 is to relate performance in each of the accounts in such a way that a net social gain or loss can be reported, coupled with an evaluation of the relative success or failure between one or more components." [15]

Scovill Manufacturing Company

The next step beyond presentation of quantitative and monetary data in relation to objectives, standards, or norms might be to arrange this information in a logical report format. One such attempt was presented in Scovill Manufacturing Company's 1972 Annual Report and titled "A Social Action Report" (Exhibit 2-3). (The format was not continued by Scovill in subsequent years.)

Some comparative quantitative information is given. For example, the report notes that the percentage of minorities employed grew from 6% in 1963 to 19% in 1972, and that women constituted about 40% of total employment in 1972. (The report would have been even more informative if some indication had been given of the extent of promotions of minorities and women into the upper ranks.)

While Scovill asserts that "the balance sheet method of reporting" was used, the main attributes of a balance sheet are lacking; that is, most items are not assigned a dollar amount, the amounts are not totaled, and assets and liabilities are not balanced. The report is rather a listing of Scovill activities and accomplishments that were judged to be socially beneficial (these are curiously labeled "assets"), along with a list of problems and areas in which better performance might be achieved. A few dollar amounts and some nonmonetary quantities are presented, but the uniqueness of the Scovill report lies mainly in the presentation of some "bads" along with the "goods."

The Scovill social report is subject to the same defect presently found in all forms of social reporting: items to be disclosed and the form of disclosure were selected by the reporting entity, subject to no generally accepted standards or independent verification. (In Chapter 6 we consider and propose standards for corporate social reporting.)

---

15 *Ibid.*

EXHIBIT 2-3

A Social Action Report: This is an admittedly imperfect attempt to report on our corporate social action. We have used the balance sheet method of reporting—not because it is possible to attach monetary values to all of the things we are doing or should be doing, but aren't—but because it allows for brevity in highlighting strengths and weaknesses in this area. We will welcome comments on the contents and on whether to continue this report.

Employment Opportunities

Assets	Liabilities
Company expansion has provided approximately 10,000 new jobs since 1963.	Fluctuating employment levels still a problem at some plant locations.
One of first members of Plans for Progress (3/17/64), a voluntary program to provide more job opportunities for minorities.	Need more upgrading of minority employees into higher labor grade jobs.
	Need more upgrading of women employees into higher labor grade jobs.
Minority employment has grown from 6% in 1963 to 19% in 1972.	Closing of Waterbury work training center after Scovill investment of $33,000. State & Federal grants to support it were terminated.
Women now constitute about 40% of total employment.	
Established National Alliance of Businessmen training program which resulted in hiring of 280 disadvantaged and 170 veterans in last 18 months in Waterbury area.	
Began first major pre-retirement counseling program for employees with U.A.W. in 1964.	
Established one of first effective alcoholism control programs for employees in 1954. (now includes drug control program)	

Environmental Controls

Assets	Liabilities
$3,500,000 Waterbury water treatment plant completed Nov. 1972.	Problem of disposing of semi-solid sludge from new Waterbury water treatment plant still being researched for a solution.
$3,000,000 air filtering systems for Waterbury mills 80% completed.	

EXHIBIT 2-3 *(Continued)*

$55,000 water treatment facility for Canadian plant completed March, 1972.

$1,100,000 water treatment facility 70% completed at Clarkesville, Ga. plant

All 10 new plants added since 1959 were built with all necessary pollution control equipment.

New brass chip dryer ($700,000) installed one year ago to reduce air pollution in Waterbury must be modified to comply with new state standards.

New OSHA (Occupational Safety and Health Act) standards may require additional expenditures.

Intermittent nitrogen dioxide emissions from Waterbury plant a problem requiring further research.

Community Involvement

Assets	Liabilities
Scovill charitable contributions averaged 1.2% of company pre-tax net income over past 5 years (1972 contributions were 8% of common stock dividends)	Programs to provide more low income housing have not been productive enough for time and money expended.

Scovill charitable contributions averaged 1.2% of company pre-tax net income over past 5 years (1972 contributions were 8% of common stock dividends)

Local non-profit group to which Scovill contributed $163,000 has sponsored 174 units of subsidized housing.

Scovill partnership with minority businessman is rebuilding 12 vacant apartments and 4 storefronts to demonstrate benefits of rehabilitating deteriorating neighborhoods.

Support other such community projects as alcohol & drug control centers, inner city parks, recreational programs, public safety committees. . . .

Employee participation in such community activities as selectmen, state representatives, school board members . . .

Scovill loaned executives to federal, state and local governments in 1972.

Programs to provide more low income housing have not been productive enough for time and money expended.

Not enough rehabilitation of inner city neighborhoods.

Still much to be accomplished in revitalizing core cities, controlling drug addiction, extending educational opportunities to the disadvantaged, etc. . . .

Failure of programs to help youth groups establish minority owned businesses after Scovill investment of $20,000.

EXHIBIT 2-3   *(Continued)*

Consumerism

Assets	Liabilities

Corporate programs utilizing more effective quality control procedures throughout the company have upgraded product performance.

"Dial NuTone" established—a nationwide telephone network to speed up service and customer communications.

NuTone added over 100 authorized service stations to its national network in the past year—and expanded its Parts & Service Dept.

NuTone simplified its product installation books and added a new Consumer Assurance Laboratory.

Hamilton Beach made its product tags more informative and simplified and clarified its warranties.

Hamilton Beach established new nationwide service organization—trained factory personnel contact independent service stations weekly to insure warranties are enforced.

New and improved procedures to upgrade quality and service to insure customer satisfaction not foolproof—problems still occur and are corrected as soon as possible.

Improver use of products despite more informative product tags and installation instructions.

Pending or future legislation which may impose more stringent standards for quality and performance.

Source: *Scovill 1972 Annual Report.* Used by permission.

Abt Associates, Inc.

Abt Associates' "Social Audit" represents one of the most ambitious social reporting efforts to date. This report has been published and bound with the corporate annual reports since 1971; the 1974 report is reproduced in full in Exhibit 2-4. The Abt approach is evaluated as a social accounting model in Chapter 3; here it is considered as an example of current social reporting.

Abt uses the unfortunate term *social audit* to describe the set of social reports. In one respect the term is appropriate: the reports do reflect an internal effort to determine the effects of the company on society. But the term *audit* has come to denote, especially within the financial community, an independent, external attestation—and the positioning of the social reports immediately following the audited financial statements would surely bring them to the attention of the financial statement readers. Further potential for confusion was created by the placement of the independent auditor's opinion between the financial statements and the social reports. The auditor's opinion does not refer to the social reports, and in earlier years the introduction to these reports noted that, "Generally accepted auditing procedures have not been developed with respect to such statements, and accordingly our independent auditors are unable to express an opinion thereon." This caveat was omitted in 1974.

Abt notes that social audits

... evaluate an organization's social impacts on its constituencies—the staff, the clients, the owners, the neighboring community, and the general public. These impacts are expressed in money units of cumulative and yearly benefits and costs.[16]

Abt believes that the social audit contributes to efficient choices among socially relevant alternatives, including alternative organizations, and alternative social programs within organizations.

The procedure used by Abt in preparing its 1974 social audit was described in some detail in 1973 and is worth quoting as an example of one way to go about this kind of self-assessment:

(1) The four major constituencies of the company (stockholders, employees, clients, and the host community) were surveyed to identify the most salient items of social concern as a basis for determining the relevant line items. In addition, the surveys served as a basis for the estimation of shadow prices for social costs and benefits for which no market values exist;

(2) The items were then quantified in terms of their dollar value; where no measurable market value for a social cost or benefit exists, shadow pricing was used.

(3) Net social incomes were computed by subtracting the sum of the social costs to each constituency from the sum of social benefits. These net social incomes are assumed to be distributed as they are created; they do not flow into the social balance sheet since such social earnings are not retained.

(4) A social equity is computed on the social balance sheet by subtracting the sum of social liabilities from the social assets.[17]

---

16 *Abt Associates Inc. Annual Report + Social Audit 1974*, p. 17.
17 *Abt Associates Inc. Annual Report + Social Audit 1973*, p. 23.

Abt Associates Inc. Social and Financial Balance Sheet

	Assets (Note 1)	1974	1973
Staff	Staff Available Within One Year (Note 2)	$ 7,555,000	6,384,000
	Staff Available After One Year (Note 3)	14,895,000	15,261,000
	Training Investment (Note 4)	2,986,000	2,051,000
		25,436,000	23,696,000
	Less Accumulated Training Obsolescence (Note 4)	1,422,000	503,000
	Total	$24,014,000	23,193,000
Organization	Creation and Development of Organization Research (Note 5)	$ 554,000	437,000
	Child Care Development	25,000	7,000
	Social Audit Development	46,000	32,000
	Total	$ 625,000	476,000
General Public and Community	Public Services Paid For Through Taxes (Net of Consumption) (Note 6)	$ 839,000	365,000
	Total	$ 839,000	365,000
Stockholders	Cash	$ 27,000	91,000
	Accounts Receivable Less Allowance for Doubtful Accounts	1,567,000	2,083,000
	Unbilled Contract Cost and Fees	1,886,000	1,789,000
	Other Current Financial Assets	169,000	42,000
	Other Long-Term Financial Assets	6,000	39,000
	Total	$ 3,655,000	4,044,000
	Physical Assets:		
	Recreation Center	$ 106,000	0
	Land and Improvements	467,000	310,000
	Buildings and Improvements	3,649,000	2,157,000
	Equipment, Furniture, and Fixtures	430,000	242,000
	Total Fixed Assets	4,652,000	2,709,000
	Less Accumulated Depreciation	336,000	204,000
	Total	$ 4,316,000	2,505,000
	Total	$33,449,000	30,583,000

Liabilities (Note 7)	1974	1973	Equity	1974	1973
Staff Wages Payable (Note 8)	**$24,014,000**	23,193,000	See statement below for staff financial equity that is not a social asset or social liability.		
	$24,014,000	23,193,000		0	0
Organizational Financing Requirement (Note 9)	**$ 1,056,000**	563,000			
	$ 1,056,000	563,000		**(431,000)**	(87,000)

Environmental Resources Used Through Pollution:

	1974	1973		1974	1973
Paper	**$ 18,000**	11,000			
Electricity	**113,000**	76,000			
Commuting	**58,000**	37,000			
	$ 189,000	124,000		**650,000**	241,000
Notes Payable (Current)	**$ 406,000**	514,000	Staff Stockholders Equity:		
Accounts Payable & Accrued Expenses	**788,000**	1,081,000	Common Stock	**95,000**	95,000
Accrued Expenses	**1,059,000**	875,000	Additional Paid-In Capital	**480,000**	480,000
Federal Income Taxes	**24,000**	109,000	Retained Earnings	**444,000**	249,000
Deferred Federal Income Taxes	**98,000**	52,000	Total	**$1,019,000**	824,000
Notes Payable (Long-Term)	**2,300,000**	1,092,000			
Leasehold Interest in Property	**130,000**	128,000	Non-Staff Stockholders Equity:		
			Common Stock	**200,000**	200,000
			Additional Paid-In Capital	**1,011,000**	1,011,000
			Retained Earnings	**936,000**	618,000
			Total	**$2,147,000**	1,829,000
	$ 4,805,000	3,851,000			
	$30,064,000	27,731,000		**$3,385,000**	2,807,000

EXHIBIT 2-4 *(Continued)*

Abt Associates Inc. Social and Financial Income Statement

Benefits	1974	1973
Company/Stockholders		
Contract Revenue and Other Income (Note 10)	$16,423,000	15,224,000
Federal Services Consumed (Note 11)	262,000	195,000
State Services Consumed	104,000	80,000
Local Services Consumed	40,000	32,000
Environmental Resources Used Through Pollution (Note 12)		
Electricity	37,000	35,000
Commuting	21,000	17,000
Paper	7,000	6,000
Total	**$16,894,000**	15,589,000
Staff		
Salaries Paid for Time Worked (Note 13)	**$ 6,231,000**	5,399,000
Career Advancement (Note 20)	700,000	602,000
Vacation and Holidays	719,000	571,000
Health and Life Insurance	461,000	361,000
Sick Leave	185,000	127,000
Retirement Income Plan	50,000	0
Parking	95,000	124,000
Tuition Reimbursement	15,000	2,000
Food Service (Note 21)	67,000	51,000
Quality of Work Space (Note 22)	134,000	16,000
Child Care	18,000	11,000
Credit Union	11,000	8,000
Recreation Center	27,000	0
Total	**$ 8,713,000**	7,272,000
Clients		
Value of Contract Research (Note 28)	**$16,423,000**	15,224,000
Professional Staff Overtime Worked But Not Paid (Note 29)	1,184,000	1,056,000
Federal Taxes Paid By Company	474,000	349,000
State and Federal Tax Worth of Net Jobs Created (Note 30)	96,000	327,000
State Taxes Paid By Company	130,000	100,000
Contribution to Knowledge (Note 31)	60,000	54,000
Total	**$18,367,000**	17,110,000
Community		
Local Taxes Paid by Company	**$ 78,000**	63,000
Local Tax Worth of Net Jobs Created	16,000	52,000
Environmental Improvements	36,000	18,000
Reduced Parking Area (Note 35)	29,000	0
Total	**$ 159,000**	133,000
Total	**$44,133,000**	40,104,000

48

Costs	1974	1973	Net Benefits	1974	1973
Salaries Paid (Exclusive of Training (Note 13) Investment and Fringe Benefits) (Note 14)	$ 5,296,000	4,319,000			
Training Investment in Staff	935,000	1,080,000			
Direct Contract Cost	5,529,000	5,596,000			
Overhead/General Administrative Expenditures Not Itemized	1,860,000	1,649,000			
Vacation and Holidays	719,000	571,000			
Improvements, Space and Environment (Note 15)	137,000	384,000			
Federal Taxes Paid (Note 16)	474,000	349,000			
State Taxes Paid (Note 16)	130,000	100,000			
Local Taxes Paid (Note 16)	78,000	63,000			
Health and Life Insurance	256,000	201,000			
Sick Leave	185,000	127,000			
Food Service	67,000	51,000			
Child Care	18,000	11,000			
Tuition Reimbursement	15,000	2,000			
Miscellaneous and Public Offering of Stock	0	154,000			
Interest Payments (Note 17)	197,000	171,000			
Income Foregone on Paid in Capital (Note 18)	265,000	276,000			
	$16,161,000	15,104,000		733,000	485,000
Opportunity Cost of Total Time Worked (Note 23)	$ 7,540,000	6,455,000			
Absence of Retirement Income Plan (Note 24)	1,000	58,000			
Layoffs and Involuntary Terminations (Note 25)	77,000	31,000			
Inequality of Opportunity (Note 26)	1,000	11,000			
Uncompensated Losses Through Theft	1,000	1,000			
Reduced Parking Area (Note 27)	29,000	0			
	$ 7,649,000	6,556,000		1,064,000	716,000
Cost of Contract Work to Client (Note 32)	$16,423,000	15,224,000			
Federal Services Consumed (Note 33)	262,000	195,000			
State Services Consumed (Note 33)	104,000	80,000			
Environmental Resources Used Through Pollution: (Note 34)					
Electricity	37,000	35,000			
Commuting	21,000	17,000			
Paper	7,000	6,000			
	$16,854,000	15,557,000		1,513,000	1,553,000
Local Services Consumed	$ 40,000	32,000			
	40,000	32,000		119,000	101,000
	$40,704,000	37,249,000		$3,429,000	2,855,000

EXHIBIT 2-4 (*Continued*)

Notes to Social Audit Statements

For more details on the calculations see the notes on the 1973 Social Audit in Abt Associates 1973 Annual Report, or write the company for detailed notes on how the Social Audit values were determined.

1. Social assets are resources which promise to provide future social or economic benefits, and are a social asset to the company valued at their present worth.

2. Staff available within one year are staff immediately available to provide research and evaluation services, estimated to be $7,555,000 for 1974 based on a discount rate of .9715 and a mean staff tenure of 2.95 years. For 1973, staff assets were valued at $6,384,000 based on a discount rate of .9604 and a mean staff tenure of 3.8 years.

3. Staff available after one year is estimated to be $14,895,000 for 1974 based on a discount rate of 1.915 and a mean staff tenure of 2.95 years. For 1973, staff assets after one year were based on a discount rate of 2.296 and a mean staff tenure of 3.8 years.

4. Training investment in staff is a social asset that promises to provide present and future benefits. The 1974 staff survey indicated that company staff spent an average 15 percent of their time in training, decreasing from a high of 25

a direct economic benefit and payment to the company.

11. Federal services consumed by the company are a social benefit to the company and the stockholders because the federal services contributed to the operations.

12. Environmental resources creating pollution are a social benefit to the company and the stockholders because the company earns economic benefits by production processes creating socially undesirable environmental effects without paying for them.

13. Salaries paid exclusive of training investment and fringe benefits are a social cost to the company and stockholders because payment for staff services reduces available company funds, and once spent for staff services these funds cannot be used again for other services.

14. Training investment in staff is a social cost to the company and stockholders which results in a loss of staff time during training and a loss of funds paid to staff during training time when the staff was non-productive.

15. Improvements, space and environment expenditures are a social and economic cost to the company and stockholders because money spent on building maintenance is not available for other uses by the company.

16. Federal, State, and Local taxes paid by the company are a social and economic cost to the company and stock-

Only four eligible staff who terminated early in the year experienced any social cost as a result of plan absence when they left.

25. Layoffs and involuntary terminations is a social cost to the staff. A survey was taken of the 72 terminees that showed that 45 percent of terminees were still unemployed after 60 days. Social cost is estimated to be one month's salary for the 40 terminees who found employment within 60 days and two months' salary for the 32 terminees who found employment after 60 days.

26. Inequality of opportunity is a social cost to the staff and is defined in terms of the costs to individuals of the income loss equal to the difference between what the minority or female individual earns and what a non-minority or male individual doing the same job with the same qualifications earns.

27. Reduced parking area is a social cost to the staff in the Cambridge office that drive automobiles. The company reduced the number of parking spaces by 80 in order to comply with Environmental Protection Agency requirements that all companies in the area reduce their parking areas.

28. Value of contract research as a social benefit is assumed to be whatever is paid for the service, since it was purchased on the open market.

29. Staff overtime worked but not paid is a social benefit to society and the client and constitutes an "invisible sub-

year.
Accumulated training obsolescence is a reduction in total training based on a straightline depreciation of training investment over the mean staff tenure.

5. Creation and development of organization is an organizational asset equated to the replacement cost of paid-in capital computed by weighing the capital stock account from 1965 to the present by the deflator for Gross Private Fixed Investment.

6. Public services paid by taxes but not consumed by the company are social assets to the general public and the community. When the company consumes fewer public services than paid by taxes, a net social asset is produced.

7. Social liabilities are sources of future economic or social cost and are valued at their present economic worth.

8. Staff wages payable are a liability contingent upon future utilization of staff on contract or administrative tasks. This amount does not constitute a liability in the legal sense but it does show expected future liability to pay staff as they provide future services.

9. Organizational financing requirements cost is equated to the difference between mean borrowing during the year and year-end borrowing which was $1,056,000 for 1974, compared to $563,000 for 1973.

10. Contract revenue and other income is a social benefit to the company and the stockholders because it results in amount of money available for other uses.

17. Interest payments are a social and economic cost to the company and stockholders because the amount spent to borrow money cannot be expensed to contract work and therefore is a loss and cannot be used for other purposes.

18. Income foregone on paid-in capital is a social and economic cost to the stockholders because of having paid-in capital tied-up in the company.

19. Salaries paid to staff for time worked is a social benefit to the staff members because it results in a direct economic benefit in payment for their contribution to company operations.

20. Career advancement is a social benefit to the staff because of the added earning power from salary increases for merit or promotion.

21. Food service subsidy by the company is a social benefit to the staff because it increases the quality of food served to the staff on the premises above that commercially available for the same prices.

22. Quality of work space is a social benefit to the staff created by the above average office space provided employees.

23. Opportunity cost of total time worked is a social cost to staff because it represents time given up while working for the company.

24. Absence of retirement plan is a social cost to the staff for 1973. In 1974 a retirement plan was implemented.

that results in a higher quality of services. The 1974 staff survey showed a decrease of overtime to 19% of regular working hours from 20% in 1973 and 33% in 1972.

30. State and federal tax worth of net jobs created are a social benefit to the general public because each new job will create additional tax revenue for the state and federal government. Expansion of the company has created 67 new jobs in Cambridge.

31. Contribution to knowledge is a social benefit to the general public because publications by the company staff constitute additions to the stock of knowledge.

32. Cost of contract research is a social cost to the client and the general public because payment for research comes from state and federal governments which reduces the amount of money available for other uses.

33. Federal and state services consumed are a social cost to the general public and society from the company's use of public services.

34. Environmental resources used through pollution are a social cost to the general public and society caused by socially undesirable effects of production that are not paid for by the company.

35. Reduced parking areas is a social benefit to the local community resulting in less pollution and traffic on the highway.

Source: *Abt Associates Inc. Annual Report + Social Audit 1974.* Used by permission.

The Abt social audit attempts to integrate social and financial effects in a balance sheet and an income statement. Although this is a commendable objective, the result is often confusing. (In Chapter 4 a different approach to such integration is proposed.)

One item is clearly understandable in the Abt reports, however; the cost of the social audit is reported at $46,000 for 1974, compared to $32,000 in 1973.

The Abt social audit can be commended for the attempt at completeness; the willingness to experiment with unproven measurement techniques; the inclusion of "bads" in the form of social costs, commitments, and obligations, along with the "goods"; and the courage to publish the whole thing, thus laying it open to attack and criticism. On the other side, it must be recognized that, however well intentioned, Abt's social report is self-serving to a consulting firm that offers to perform social audits for a fee. Indeed, an earlier report was accompanied by a promotional letter noting, "We have been developing the social audit for several years and are now able to offer a program of social measurement services to both private and public organizations."

Phillips Screw Company

The preceding examples of social reporting were prepared by the reporting companies with no external check or verification. In contrast, Phillips Screw Company engaged outside consultants to perform an independent study of the firm's environmental impact. The consultants' report, which was published in Phillips' annual report for the fiscal year ending March 31, 1973 (but not in 1974), is reproduced in Exhibit 2-5. This "pollution audit" is unique in several respects: it was performed by external, independent consultants; it was published by the company even though several liabilities were reported; and this voluntary disclosure occurred in a year when the company reported a substantial net loss. The pollution audit was not mentioned in the report of Phillips' independent CPAs.

This sampling of social reporting in corporate annual reports reveals a variety of practices. Most of these are simple narrative disclosures of positive corporate actions in areas of social concern, but they range through the reporting of quantitative information to the presentation of a complex, detailed "social audit."

Special Reports

The annual report is not the only vehicle for social reporting; the Corson and Steiner, and Jarett studies cited earlier found that 17% and 11%, respec-

EXHIBIT 2-5   Pollution Audit

The information herein has been extracted from a comprehensive pollution audit conducted by the undersigned on the Phillips Screw Company subsidiary Phillips Metallurgical, Inc. (PMI) and its subsidiary, Shell Cast Corp. (SCC).

The audit included consideration of air, water, noise and solid waste effluents and consisted of engineering and economic segments. Preliminary technical equipment needs and costs were projected to provide management with parameters for determining the economic impact on the Company and its operations. Experience suggests that these preliminary cost estimates will prove to be within normally accepted deviation ranges.

Where required, effluent testing was conducted in accordance with standardized techniques applicable to the circumstances encountered at each site. For the business/economic analysis, not presented in this summary, Company financial data on PMI and SCC were provided and integrated with proposed abatement equipment capital and operating costs as estimated by the undersigned.

Based upon our technical and economic analysis, the following significant conclusions have been drawn: PMI has two effluent liabilities.

1. The plant exceeds Vermont air pollution standards—particulate emissions calculated at 7.0 lbs/hr compared to a maximum allowable level of 2.8 lbs/hr.

2. The plant exceeds Federal OSHA air contaminant standards—particulate concentration of at 25.2 mg/m^3 compared to a maximum allowable level of 10.0 mg/m^3.

SCC has two effluent liabilities.

1. The plant exceeds Connecticut air pollution standards—particulate emissions calculated at 3.0 lbs/hr compared to a maximum allowable level of 1.53 lbs/hr.

2. The plant emits at the Federal OSHA air contaminant standard—particulate concentration of at 10.0 mg/m^3 compared to a maximum allowable level of 10 mg/m^3.

No effluent liabilities in the areas of water, solid waste or noise pollution were observed.

Financial liabilities are as follows:

1. PMI to meet State and Federal air pollution standards requires a capital investment of $32,500 and annual operating expenses of $3,700.

2. SCC to meet State and Federal air pollution standards requires a capital investment of $25,500 and annual operating expenses of $3,200. (These estimated costs are before tax and do not include amortization of capital equipment.)

In our opinion, expenditures of the levels cited for a remedial program of air pollution control will bring the current foundry operations into compliance with the respective State and Federal standards as they now exist. Furthermore, these expenditures are expected to provide sufficient margin to permit continued compliance in the event of any change in air pollution standards which we consider reasonably forseeable. Additionally, the nature and volume of solid waste effluents from current operations provide a sufficient margin for continued compliance in the event of reasonable changes to those standards.

Resource Planning Associates, Inc.

Cambridge, Mass.
June 1, 1973

Source: *Phillips Screw Company Annual Report 1973.* Used by permission.

53

tively, of the responding companies used a "special report" for public disclosure of information on social responsibility.

As might be expected, great variety is found among such special reports. They may appear at random intervals and in response to varying corporate objectives. The examples reviewed in the following paragraphs suggest the diversity of purposes, coverage, content, and form.

General Motors Corporation's *1973 Report on Progress in Areas of Public Concern* is, at 96 pages, one of the longest reports available, with sections on automotive safety, pollution control, emission control, energy conservation, research, product quality, employee development, and operations in South Africa. This document, liberally illustrated with photographs and drawings, is essentially a report of a conference held by GM to "report its progress in several areas of public concern" and attended by a number of institutional GM stockholders and other individuals. Despite the report's length, there is little in the way of specific information. For example, "significant progress" is claimed in air-pollution control and some examples are given, but no overall, companywide data are provided; and the report notes that, "GM plants salvage about 120,000 tons a year of cardboard and paper," but no information is given as to the quantity *not* salvaged or the total quantity used to provide a basis for comparison. The company does report the amount spent on industrial pollution control ($58 million in 1972, $80 million projected in 1973), and information on the progress of various projects and technical efforts is good although subjective.

Overall, GM's report is weak in that it tells us little about the damage done by the company and its products or the costs incurred and imposed on society. It is often defensive in tone and is used excessively as a propaganda vehicle against new and tougher controls:

> The role of the automobile in air pollution is frequently misunderstood. It is not the sole contributor as some ecology buffs would have you to believe.
>
> For too long, the businessman has been maligned and misinterpreted and mistaken for an exploiter of society instead of a contributor to society.

There is one major exception to these critical comments—the two pages devoted to employment of minorities and women. To be adequate, information reported in this area should include present totals as a percentage of the appropriate work force categories as well as an indication of the degree of change over time; otherwise the reader cannot intelligently evaluate the company's position or performance. In this respect, GM's report is quite complete regarding minorities and women in relation to total employment and employment in white-collar jobs; the data for professional, management, and technical positions are less complete but still informative. (Apparently in an effort to reach a liberal audience, GM included most of this same information in a four-page ad in an early 1974 issue of *The New Republic*.) The company's programs and efforts to recruit minorities and women are also fully described.

If GM's report, for all its length, was incomplete, defensive, and sprinkled with propaganda, ITT's 1973 publication *Serving People* was blatantly self-serving. This 32-page, slick-paper and full-color document (perhaps two-thirds photographs) was received (unsolicited) at a time when ITT was in the news almost daily over alleged attempts to stop antitrust proceedings through contributions to President Nixon's reelection campaign, and alleged attempts to persuade the Central Intelligence Agency to help bring about the downfall of Chile's President Allende.

Equal opportunity; operations in South Africa; an ITT-sponsored Minority Enterprise Small Business Investment Company (MESBIC); the environment; product quality; youth programs; and assistance to the arts, education, and the handicapped are among the programs discussed. Generally two or three cases are briefly discussed for each program, giving an impression of involvement but no indication of the extent of the company's overall impact. Indeed, there are virtually no companywide figures, percentages, or the like. Nothing negative is presented, nor is the information susceptible to any kind of analysis or rational evaluation. When a company sets out to overcome an unfavorable image by convincing the public that "we are involved," with no desire to provide a complete report of the company's social impact, warts and all, we can expect an effort like ITT's.

United States Steel and Bank of America have both produced reports that contrast rather strikingly with GM's and ITT's. These reports are relatively short (15 and 18 pages) with unjustified type and no pictures or fancy covers. The US Steel report deals with jobs for the socially disadvantaged, aid to education, urban housing and transportation, environmental control (although the only meaningful information given is the amount spent for pollution-control facilities), charitable contributions, employee involvement in community affairs, and the impact of the company's basic operations on society. The inclusion of this last topic in social reports is surprisingly rare. Some companies seem to ignore the substantial social impact of their basic operations, apparently believing that this impact is "economic" rather than "social." But if it is to be complete, social accounting must take into account *all* effects of an organization on society; attempts to separate the economic and noneconomic effects are usually arbitrary and often futile.

The Bank of America report focuses primarily on the areas of housing, minorities, the environment, and social unrest. Various bank programs are classified under these four topics and briefly described. The result is essentially an inventory of Bank of America programs having significant social dimensions.

The Bank of America report was prepared primarily for dissemination to bank employees. While a separate report was used in this case, numerous other companies have used the house organ or company magazine to inform employees of company social programs and efforts. A particularly good example is *The Quaker,* published by the Quaker Oats Company, whose recent issues contained articles on air- and water-pollution control efforts, resources recovery (recycling), safety, grants from the company foundation, and voluntary community services by individual employees.

Numerous other individual special reports could be cited, but those mentioned are good examples. This approach to social reporting is characterized by little uniformity in style, content, or coverage. Individual cases or examples are often briefly described, and occasionally absolute amounts or quantities are encountered. The tone is invariably positive and optimistic. Shortcomings are practically never mentioned; goals are seldom described; quantification is rare and generally restricted to absolute amounts at some point in time, with no indication of percentages or rates of change. No bases for comparison are provided, and consequently all but the most knowledgeable readers are left with no rational way of evaluating the reporting company's social impact.

SOCIAL ACCOUNTING IN THE PUBLIC SECTOR

Private-sector entities—at least profit-seeking ones—can be evaluated in terms of economic results. Net profit, return on investment, and earnings per share are measures readily obtained from traditional financial reports. These measures are useful for evaluation of private-sector entities because the primary objective of these companies is to earn a profit.

Public-sector entities are not profit seeking within the usually accepted meaning of the word *profit.* They do seek other objectives, of course, and it has thus been necessary to develop alternative means of measuring and evaluating the performance of entities in the public sector. In response to this need, a substantial body of knowledge and a collection of techniques have accumulated for social accounting in the public sector.

To even begin to cover public-sector social accounting would extend this book well beyond a reasonable length. Although such a discussion is beyond our scope, the reader may wish to consult such sources as current government publications, *The Federal Accountant,* and the recent anthology *Accounting for Social Goals,* by John Leslie Livingstone and Sanford C. Gunn (Harper & Row, 1974), for more on this important aspect of social accounting.

SUMMARY

This chapter reviews internal corporate social accounting and external reporting. Much is being done, and many different approaches are being used. Perhaps this is justified by the diversity of the American economy, or perhaps it merely reflects the immaturity of social accounting and the lack of communication among those interested in the phenomenon.

Internal social accounting ranges from the simple and inexpensive to the involved, complicated, and costly sort of activity carried on at Bank of America. Motivations for internal social accounting also run a gamut, although the main objective seems to be simply to find out what the company is actually doing, indicating that corporate information systems do not presently provide relevant information on costs and effects of corporate social activities.

External social reporting appears primarily in the annual report, but a significant number of companies use a separate special report. Both approaches are usually characterized by an optimistic tone; little or no mention of detriments to society; inadequate quantification; and no bases for comparison and evaluation in the form of norms, averages, standards, or ratios. Except for the Phillips Screw Company's Pollution Audit, there is no independent attestation such as that provided by a CPA, even though disclosure frequently appears in the annual report and in some cases, most notably Abt Associates, Inc., and Scovill Manufacturing Company, appears in a format resembling that used for traditional financial statements. One can only speculate about the potential for confusion on the part of readers and for liability suits against CPAs.

Several models have been developed that purport to be generally applicable to social reporting. In a sense these are now competing in the marketplace. Should any one be adopted by a significant number of companies, the anarchic diversity described in this chapter would diminish and we might begin to see some degree of order and comparability in corporate social accounting.

Chapter 3 describes several of these models, and a comprehensive reporting model is then proposed in Chapter 4.

*That fellow seems to me to possess but one
idea, and that is a wrong one.*

Samuel Johnson, in Boswell's Life of Dr. Johnson.

3   Proposed Approaches to Corporate Social Accounting

Suppose that a chief executive officer has decided to take into account information concerning his firm's social programs and social performance for internal resource allocation and employee evaluations. He is also considering possible public disclosure of this information to silence critics and as an act of corporate citizenship. What kind of informational report could he call for?

The previous chapter partially answers this question by presenting the approaches of several corporations that have attempted some form of social accounting. This chapter considers and evaluates several *proposed* approaches to social accounting and reporting that cover a wide range of complexity, costliness, and disclosure.

EXTENSION OF FINANCIAL STATEMENTS

One approach to social reporting is to add information within the format of present financial statements. This may be done through narrative disclosures or through the addition of new accounts.

Narrative Disclosure

The simplest method of reporting social information is through narrative disclosure. The American Accounting Association's Committee on Environmental Effects of Organization Behavior has proposed an extension of the current attested financial reporting model to include certain environmental disclosures; presumably these disclosures would appear in footnotes to the attested financial statements. The Committee called for *verbal descriptions* of the following:

1. Identification of environmental problems—specific organizational problems with regard to control, imposed control standards, compliance deadlines, penalties for noncompliance, environmental considerations contained in executory contracts, and other contingent aspects.
2. Abatement goals of the organization—detailed description of plans for abatement, projection of time schedules, estimates of costs and/or budgeted expenditures.
3. Progress of the organization—description of tangible progress, cost to date, expected future costs and pertinent nonmonetary information relative to the organization's attainment of environmental goals.
4. Disclosure of material environmental effects on financial position, earnings and business activities of the organization.[1]

The recommended disclosure would provide information useful not only to those members of the public concerned with environmental matters, but also to investors interested in potential future liabilities and assessments that might result from the problems and progress reported. Further, the process of putting together the suggested information would be informative to management and would go a long way toward satisfying the primary management objectives of a "social audit" cited in Chapter 2.

Quantitative information tends to be more informative and more useful than nonquantitative information; the committee's recommendation appears to contemplate largely nonquantiative disclosure. This modest approach may be an appropriate first step toward a goal of more sophisticated and quantified disclosure, and is understandable in view of the committee's professed concern with recommending a procedure that would be acceptable to the accounting profession. This desire for acceptability may also have been at least partially responsible for restraining the committee from straying from its charge to consider organizational effects on the *physical environment*; nevertheless, narrative information about discriminatory practices and progress, health and safety aspects of products and employment, and other social accounting matters is also useful.

In sum, the AAA Committee's recommendation for verbal disclosure of envi-

---

1 "Report of the Committee on Environmental Effects of Organization Behavior." *The Accounting Review*, Supplement to Vol. XLVIII, 1973, p. 110.

ronmental effects, attested to by independent auditors, would result in presentation of clearly useful information that, though not as complete or as quantitative as many might wish, would have a chance of early acceptance by the accounting profession because of its simplicity.

Additional Accounts

Floyd Beams has proposed recognition in the accounts of industrial site deterioration caused by pollution.[2]

According to Beams, delayed site maintenance of prior years would seem to qualify as a prior-period adjustment, in accordance with Accounting Principles Board Opinion No. 9. The charge would be to Retained Earnings, with an offsetting credit to a new account called Allowance for Industrial Site Deterioration, a contra-asset deducted from the Land account. *Current* site deterioration would be similarly recognized by a charge to an expense account, Industrial Site Deterioration, and a credit to the allowance.

The Allowance for Industrial Site Deterioration could be reduced (or charged) when outlays are made to reestablish a deteriorated plant site. Other current outlays, made to *maintain* the industrial site by controlling pollution and disposing of industrial waste, could be charged to a new expense account called Industrial Site Maintenance.

Financial statements reflecting Beam's proposals might look like those in Exhibit 3-1. The essential differences between these and ordinary financial statements are (*1*) certain expenses otherwise reflected in a variety of cost accounts are collected in the account Industrial Site Maintenance; (*2*) deterioration of the industrial site is reflected in a reduction in the book value of Land and in a new expense, Industrial Site Deterioration; and (*3*) Retained Earnings may be charged for previously unrecognized site deterioration.

Beams notes that the AICPA's *Auditing Standards and Procedures* (republished as *Statement on Auditing Standards*) calls for qualification of the auditor's opinion for material uncertainties, and that auditors therefore may have to consider the potential financial effects of serious antipollution law violations. A qualification due to such uncertainty might appear as follows:

In our opinion, subject to any future assessments and charges, presently undeterminable, that may result from past and current environmental

---

2 Floyd A. Beams, "Accounting for Environmental Pollution," *The New York Certified Public Accountant* (now *The CPA Journal*), August 1970, pp. 657–661.

damage, the accompanying financial statements fairly present the financial position of XYZ Company at December 31, 19___, and the results of its operations and the changes in its financial position for the year then ended, in conformity with generally accepted accounting principles applied on a basis consistent with that of the preceding year.

The Beams proposal would appear to be most applicable for firms engaged in strip-mining, agribusiness, resort development and management, and other industries in which the condition of the soil, land surface, and still bodies of water is an important factor. For such industries this extension and modification of traditional financial statements should be practical, moderately informative, and auditable; indeed, it could probably be accommodated within present generally acceptable accounting principles. On the other hand, the Beams proposal would appear to have limited relevance for accounting for the effects of air pollution and water pollution of *flowing* waterways. Particularly heavy emissions into the air can damage local soil and plant life; most effluents, however, appear to drift away from the offending plant site to settle elsewhere or become trapped in the atmosphere (where they might eventually cause damage by blocking the sun's rays). Likewise, flowing rivers and streams can cleanse themselves within a reasonably short time after water pollution is discontinued, and consequently it appears unnecessary to recognize any *long-term* deterioration of the polluter's assets. Neither of these arguments holds, and Beams' proposal becomes more relevant when a number of industrial concerns are collectively generating air or water pollution such that the reporting company is unable to renew its site solely through its own actions.

The AAA Committee on Environmental Effects of Organization Behavior, cited previously, also suggested the use of additional accounts for environmental disclosures. Like Beams, the Committee recommended that environmental control expenses be collected in a new, separate account in the income statement; it also proposed separate disclosure of environmental control expenditures in the statement of sources and application of funds, and separate classification on the balance sheet for environmental control facilities and related depreciation. But the most important modification proposed would reflect liabilities for future pollution-control outlays arising out of past transactions, in place of the present practice of footnote disclosure. The Committee listed three examples of these liabilities:

1. The liability for assessed but unpaid penalties or pollution taxes for non-compliance with standards.

EXHIBIT 3-1

XYZ Company
Balance Sheet
December 31, 19__

Current Assets			$xxx
Fixed Assets			
Land (Note 1)	$xxx		
Less Allowance for Industrial Site			
Deterioration (Note 2)	xxx	$xxx	
Buildings and Equipment	$xxx		
Less Allowance for Depreciation	xxx	xxx	xxx
			$xxx
Current Liabilities			$xxx
Long-Term Liabilities			xxx
Stockholders' Equity			xxx
			$xxx

XYZ Company
Statement of Income and Retained Earnings
For the Year Ended December 31, 19__

Sales			$xxx
Production Costs			
Materials	$xxx		
Labor	xxx		
Depreciation	xxx		
Industrial Site Deterioration (Note 2)	xxx		
Industrial Site Maintenance (Note 3)	xxx		
Other Production Costs	xxx	$xxx	
Nonproduction Costs		xxx	xxx
Net Income from Operations			$xxx
Provision for Income Taxes			xxx
Net Income to Retained Earnings			$xxx
Retained Earnings, January 1, 19__			xxx
			$xxx
Less: Dividends	$xxx		
Delayed Industrial Site Maintenance	xxx		xxx
(Note 4)			
Retained Earnings, December 31, 19__			$xxx

2. The liability for estimated penalty or tax (not assessed) for noncompliance with standards or deadlines.

3. The liability for the estimated cost of voluntary "restoration" of the environment for past or current damages.

These examples raise some questions. The first liability is already generally recognized and reported; perhaps the Committee merely had separate disclosure in mind. The second example is theoretically sound under present generally accepted accounting principles, although it would be difficult to induce corporations to report such a liability fully and fairly. The third example does not appear to fit any generally accepted notion of a liability; it is at best a *commitment*, which might warrant footnote or parenthetical disclosure but no formal recognition in the accounts.

Basically it appears that the Committee would like all amounts associated with environmental matters to be separately disclosed in newly created accounts. This is a modest enough proposal and is certainly consistent with the doctrine of full disclosure, which implies modification and reclassification of accounts as conditions change and different information needs arise. When considered in conjunction with the Committee's recommendation for narrative disclosure, discussed earlier in this chapter, these changes in traditional financial statements should provide useful and perhaps sufficient information on the reporting entity's effect on the physical environment. Of course readers might desire information about other social effects, but as noted earlier, the Committee's charge mentioned only effects on the physical environment.

Notes to Exhibit 3-1

Note 1: In addition to the exchange price, Land is charged with outlays incurred to restore acquired sites to an acceptable level.

Note 2: Deterioration of the industrial site that has taken place during the current accounting period is recorded as a charge to Industrial Site Deterioration expense and credited to the Allowance for Industrial Site Deterioration. Outlays to reestablish a deteriorated plant site are charged to the Allowance for Industrial Plant Deterioration.

Note 3: Industrial Site Maintenance is charged for current outlays that are made to maintain the industrial site by controlling pollution and disposing of industrial waste.

Note 4: Retained Earnings has been charged for deterioration of the industrial site that occurred in prior years but was not previously recorded; the credit was to Allowance for Industrial Site Deterioration.

PROPOSALS FOR NEW REPORTING FORMATS

Much of the interest in corporate social reporting is in the development of new and distinctive reporting formats or models. Present financial statements appear to be too constrained by format and tradition to accommodate the kinds of social information many feel should be reported. Proposed models range from Marlin's one-dimensional statement, which is restricted to physical information about pollution, to the complex statements of Abt and Seidler, which present in monetary terms information on several dimensions of social concern.

Marlin's Pollution Reports

John Tepper Marlin has proposed two approaches to reporting on a company's pollution.[3] One report (Exhibit 3-2) would compare the company's controls (presumably as of some date to be indicated) with state-of-the-art standards that Marlin would have established jointly by an industry committee and the AICPA's committees on environmental accounting and social measurement. Marlin also suggests the following addition to the auditor's opinion to cover this report by a paper manufacturer:

> In addition to the financial statements, we have examined to the extent considered necessary in the circumstances all assertions in this report regarding the company's compliance with environmental regulations and the adequacy of its existing and planned pollution control equipment. In our opinion these assertions are consistent with independent inquiries made with regulatory authorities, equipment suppliers and outside scientific consultants; with inspection of company records of equipment purchased and periodic efficiency ratings; and with state-of-the-art standards developed by the AICPA committees on environmental accounting and social measurement and the committee on pollution control of the American Paper Institute.[4]

(Marlin notes that the referenced American Paper Institute committee is presently only hypothetical.)

Marlin proposes a second report, to accompany the first, to present actual pollution emissions figures along with certain relevant federal standards. An

---

3 John Tepper Marlin, "Accounting for Pollution," *The Journal of Accountancy,* February 1973, pp. 41–46.
4 *Ibid.,* p. 44.

EXHIBIT 3-2 State-of-the-Art Pollution Control Report for Ideal Paper Co.: Production, Water Use and Pollution Control of Mill

Location	Production (Tons/Day) Pulp	Other	Water Use (Million Gals/Day)	Pollution Control Adequacy Water Primary	Secondary	Tertiary	Air Gas and Odor	Part.
Mill A	1600	1750	89	✓	✓	X	✓	X
Mill B	1200	970	95	✓	'73	X	✓	X
Mill C	1200	1100	82	✓	'73	'73	'74	✓
Mill D	610	840	40	'74	'75	X	X	✓
Mill E	0	1395	61	✓	—	—	—	✓
Total*	4610	6055	367	80%	25%	0%	50%	60%
				86.8%	34.7%	0%	60.7%	39.3%

Note: Presently adequate (state-of-the-art) pollution controls are indicated by a check mark (✓), inadequate controls by an (X). A dash (—) means equipment is not needed. Where adequate equipment is being installed, the expected year of completion is indicated.

* Two summary figures are given. The first line is the percentage of plants which now have adequate controls. The second line is the proportion of pulp production which is adequately controlled. It is obtained by adding up pulp capacity of adequately controlled plants and dividing this by total pulp production of all plants requiring controls.

Source: John Tepper Marlin, "Accounting for Pollution," *The Journal of Accountancy,* February 1973, p. 43. Copyright © 1973 by the American Institute of Certified Public Accountants, Inc. Used by permission.

example of this report is presented in Exhibit 3-3, which gives emissions for three New York paper plants. He also suggests that this second report could be covered in the following extension of the auditor's opinion:

> In addition to Company B's financial statements, we have examined to the extent considered necessary in the circumstances its assertions regarding the amount of pollution caused by its mills. In our opinion, based on consultation with plant staff and governmental authorities, and on an independent sampling of emissions by a private environmental consulting firm, the reported emissions fairly reflect the pollution caused by the mills at the time of our investigation, and the company has budgeted adequate operating expenses to maintain this level of control.[5]

Marlin's reports could be generalized to produce a separate report on each area of significant social concern, reflecting state-of-the-art standards where these could be specified and actual performance in relation to appropriate performance standards. The resulting reports would be covered in the auditor's opinion.

The Marlin approach is commendable in four important respects: it focuses on measures that are not hypothetical but are actually being made today; it calls for reporting of *standards* that, because of the way in which they would be established, should have some degree of general acceptance; it is flexible enough to allow for recognition of changing social concerns (a separate report could be prepared for each area of concern); and the reporting firm's independent CPA would attest to the information disclosed. There are also some significant drawbacks: achieving concensus on appropriate standards would be difficult, although not impossible; such standards would have to be developed for each industry and for each major area of social concern (and these concerns may change within fairly short periods of time); several reports of a single firm on various aspects of social performance cannot readily be integrated to produce an overall rating or evaluation; and audit fees would dramatically increase, resulting in an increased cost to the public (through higher product prices), which might be greater than the pollution or other detriment involved.

Overall, Marlin's proposal would appear to be fairly practical, at least with respect to pollution, and would result in information that would fall short of the desires and needs of some but would be valuable to many. The effort involved in developing the information to be reported would likely stimulate a

---

5 *Ibid.*, p. 45.

EXHIBIT 3-3   **Sample Net Pollution Emissions and Federal Standards: By Type of Pollutant***

	Company A	Company B	Company C (Tissue Manufacturer)			Federal Drinking Water Standards	
			#1 White Water Tank	#1 Sewer	Pulping Area Floor Drain	Desirable	Permissible
	(NSSC Pulp)	(Kraft Pulp)					
Production (tons/day)	70	550	170	170	170	—	—
Flow ('000 gals./day)	5,000	1900	127	410	23	—	—
A. Biochemical Oxygen Demand	344	18	93	156	234	(8)	(14)
Chemical oxygen demand	1,742	110	46	254	573	?	?
Solids, dissolved	1,454	478	3	114	28	200	500
Solids, suspended	264	21	16	170	399	(6)	(10)
B. Color	40	220	0	12	7	10	75.
Coliform bacteria	760,000	20	0	0	1900	100	10,000
Phenols	45	0	2	5	4	0	0.001
Sulfate	9	186	-0.8	0.2	3	50	250
Chloride	15	388	0.7	0.5	3	25	250
Copper	15	0	35	30	25	0	1
Lead	0	0	-12	-9	2	0	0.05
Zinc	-50	0.02	1498	20	22	0	5

* Question marks indicate missing source figures.

Source: John Tepper Marlin, "Accounting for Pollution," *The Journal of Accountancy*, February 1973, p. 45. Copyright © 1973 by the American Institute of Certified Public Accountants, Inc. Used by permission.

EXHIBIT 3-4

Utility Company is a gas and electric firm operating in the midwestern United States. Its rates and return on investment are regulated by a state utility commission. The company operates exclusively within a single state, although it receives natural gas and coal from outside the state's borders.

This SRAR has been prepared to measure Utility Company's response to current social concerns. The data contained in this report are true and accurate within the current limits of scientific measurement techniques available for research of this type. Each of the elements attempts to convey to the reader information that may be useful in his social evaluation of the company.

The data were developed as a result of a social audit of the Utility Company. X-Y-Z Associates, an independent research organization, conducted the audit and prepared the following SRAR. Financing for this research project was provided by a midwestern university.

X-Y-Z Associates, Inc.

Source: Steven C. Dilley and Jerry J. Weygandt, "Measuring Social Responsibility: An Empirical Test," *The Journal of Accountancy,* September 1973, p.64. Copyright © 1973 by the American Institute of Certified Public Accountants, Inc. Used by permission.

good deal of corrective action, and this might be an implicit objective of Marlin's proposal.

Dilley and Weygandt's Social Responsibility Annual Report

Marlin's approach is extended by Steven Dilley and Jerry Weygandt to cover not only pollution but also health and safety matters, along with minority recruitment and promotion; outlays in these areas would also be disclosed.[6] Information largely available in required government reports and elsewhere would be presented in a set of statements unrelated to each other except for the listing of outlays in the several areas. These statements are presented in Exhibits 3-4 through 3-11.

Dilley and Weygandt used an actual Midwestern gas and electric utility company to illustrate their proposed approach. They note that different statements would be required for firms in different industries.

The first statement, Exhibit 3-4, is an analog to the independent auditor's opinion on financial statements. This statement presumes that the "social audit" is performed not by the reporting company but by some independent third party. The next two statements, Exhibits 3-5 and 3-6, describe the com-

6 Steven C. Dilley and Jerry J. Weygandt, "Measuring Social Responsibility: An Empirical Test," *The Journal of Accountancy,* September 1973, pp. 62–70.

EXHIBIT 3-5

Type of company: Gas-electric public utility
1971 operating revenues: $40,000,000
1971 operating income: $ 5,500,000

	Residential	Industrial and commercial	Government and institutional	Misc.
Electric sales revenue (%)	40.0	46.5	8.5	5.0
Number of electric customers	66,000	10,000	40	2
Gas sales revenue (%)	48.0	50.0	—	2.0
Number of gas customers	41,000	6,500	—	5

Number of employees:
Subject to union agreements — 360
Supervisors and professional staff — 140
Total — 500
Percent of community population — .17%

Age of company: 60 years

Average salary of employees:
Subject to union agreements — $10,650
Supervisors and professional staff — $13,500

	Total	Community*
Common stockholders:	9,000	5,000

Number of stockholders holding greater than 5 percent of outstanding shares: None

Subsidiary companies owned: None

Stock investments in nonsubsidiary companies: None

* State in which company is located.
Source: Dilley and Weygandt, p. 65.

69

EXHIBIT 3-6

Area in square miles:	700
Population	300,000
Minority group (blacks), % of population:	1.1%
Type:	Urban-suburban, some rural.
Location:	Midwestern U.S.
Economic base:	Industrial, government services.
Physical characteristics:	Rolling plains.
Weather characteristics:	Large seasonal variations in temperature; substantial yearly precipitation.
Number of government units:	50
Median family income:	$11,000
Population— Earning less than poverty level (%):	5.4%
Earning more than $15,000 (%):	27.2%

Source: Dilley and Weygandt, p. 66.

pany and its community. This information is offered to establish perspective and to provide the reader with some basis for evaluation of performance, since the definition of relevant social activities may vary by the type of company and by the characteristics and needs of the community.

The next two statements, Exhibits 3-7 and 3-8, report on air pollution, thermal pollution, and water consumption. (Note the similarity in form of this information to that presented in Marlin's report of emissions by paper companies, Exhibit 3-3.) The data in these schedules are derived largely from statistics in Federal Power Commission Form No. 67 ("Steam-Electric Plant Air and Water Quality Control Data"), Environmental Protection Agency emission factors, and federal and state pollution standards.

The information on occupation health and safety presented in Exhibit 3-9 is adapted from a report that must be filed under the Occupational Safety and Health Act of 1970. Data on recruitment and promotion of minorities and women are presented in Exhibit 3-10; this report combines information required in the Equal Employment Opportunity Commission's Form EEO-1 with other readily available information.

The only attempt at integration of social information is contained in Exhibit 3-11, which reports funds expended on pollution control and environmental protection, charitable contributions, and certain employee fringe benefits. Following a suggestion of the Council on Economic Priorities, the total is compared to company advertising expenses and total revenues. Presumably, outlays for special minority recruitment and advancement programs would be reported here except that this utility company made no such outlays during the reporting period (see Exhibit 3-10). Outlays for health and safety programs are probably omitted because of the difficulty in isolating such expenditures.

The Dilley and Weygandt proposal merits consideration because the information it calls for would not only be useful to a corporation's various publics but could also be obtained at little effort or expense. There is a fair degree of quantification, including certain monetary figures, and some bases for evaluation are provided. The proposal that the reports be prepared by independent

EXHIBIT 3-7*

		Particulate matter	
	Coal	Oil	Gas
1971	3.3717	0.003	0.111
1970	4.3920	0.001	0.095
		Sulfur oxides	
	Coal	Oil	Gas
1971	17.71	0.046	0.005
1970	22.22	0.027	0.004
		Nitrogen oxides	
	Coal	Oil	Gas
1971	2.69	NA†	NA
1970	3.58	NA	NA

* The company was in compliance with all state and federal laws in regard to air pollution during 1971. Federal air pollution emission standards generally apply to new power plants. No new coal-fired boilers were put in service during 1971. State regulations require compliance with stringent air pollution standards by 1973. To meet those more stringent standards, the company will have to reduce its pollution emissions by 1973. To accomplish this goal, the company is installing electrostatic precipitators to trap 99.5 percent of the particulate matter, using as much natural gas as is available and using low-sulfur coal when it can be obtained. The pollutants emitted during 1971 can impose social costs upon the community which the company serves. These social costs are composed of increased soiling costs, increased incidence of respiratory disease and decreases in property values.
† Not applicable.
Source: Dilley and Weygandt, p. 66.

EXHIBIT 3-8

Type of cooling system: Once-through
Source of cooling water: Fresh-water lake, area 5.4 sq. mi.
Cooling water data:

	Temperature as received	Temperature as discharged	Difference
Winter maximum	40°F	69°F	29°F
Summer maximum	79°F	105°F	26°F
Average rate of water consumption during 1971:	1 cu ft/sec		
Average rate of water withdrawal from water body:	152 cu ft/sec		
Average rate of water discharge to water body:	151 cu ft/sec		
Depth of water withdrawal:	17 ft		
Depth of water discharge:	Surface		

Source: Dilley and Weygandt, p. 67.

72

EXHIBIT 3-9*

Average number of employees during the period:	500
Total hours worked by all employees:	403,000
On-the-job fatalities during the period:	None
Number of workdays lost due to on-the-job injuries:	35
Number of employees affected:	6
% of total employees:	1.2%
Number of workdays lost due to occupational illness:	0
Number of employees affected:	0
% of total employees:	0%

* The data for this statement were derived from OSHA Form No. 103. The information contained on that report is required by the Williams-Steiger Occupational Health and Safety Act. The initial reporting period ran from July 1, 1971, to December 31, 1971. Subsequent reporting periods will run from January 1 to December 31 of each year.
Source: Dilley and Weygandt, p. 68.

EXHIBIT 3-10

Total population of community:	300,000
% minorities:	1.1%
Total number of employees	500
Total number of minority Negro and Spanish-surnamed employees:	9
Subject to union contracts:	8
% of all employees subject to union contracts:	2.2%
% of all employees:	1.6%
Supervisory and professional staff:	1
% of all supervisory and professional staff:	0.7%
% of all employees:	0.2%
Total number of female employees:	83
Subject to union contracts:	71
% of all employees subject to union contracts:	19.9%
% of all employees:	14.2%
Supervisory and professional staff:	12
% of all supervisory and professional staff:	8.6%
% of all employees:	2.4%
Special minority recruitment and advancement programs:	
Negroes and Spanish-surnamed employees:	None
dollars spent:	$0
Females:	None
dollars spent:	$0

Source: Dilley and Weygandt, p. 68.

EXHIBIT 3-11

Environmental

Installation of electrostatic precipitators (Note 1)		$ 26,000
Construction of power plants (Note 2)		2,089,000
Construction of transmission lines (Note 3)		35,000
Electrical substation beautification (Note 4)		142,000
Incremental cost of low-sulfur coal (Note 5)		33,670
Conversion of service vehicles to use of propane gas (Note 6)		3,700
Incremental cost of underground electric installations (Note 7)		737,000
Incremental cost of silent jackhammers (Note 8)		100
Environmental research—		
Thermal	$17,000	
Nuclear	1,955	
Other	38,575	
		57,530
Subtotal		
Total environmental funds flow		$3,124,000

Other benefits

Charitable contributions		$26,940
Employee educational and recreational expenditures (Note 9)		6,000
Total other benefits		32,940
Total 1971 funds flow for socially relevant activities		$3,156,940
As a percentage of 1971 operating revenues		7.9%
As a percentage of 1971 advertising expenses		8,500%

Notes to funds statement

1 The company will complete installation of two electrostatic precipitators in 1973. Costs in 1971 totaled $26,000

2 The company is building power plants which will begin operation in the middle to late 1970's. Incremental cash costs of environmental controls installed in these plants during 1971 totaled $2,089,000.

3 The company is constructing a high-voltage transmission line from another community to the company's service area. Environmental cash costs resulting from wider spacing of line towers totaled $35,000 in 1971.

4 The company constructed a new substation in 1971 with an enclosed structure rather than open exposure of the electric transformers. The cost of this enclosure along with landscaping of existing substations totaled $142,000 in 1971.

5 The company used approximately 150,000 tons of coal during 1971 for electric power generation. Low-sulfur content coal comprised 8.6 percent of this coal consumption with the remaining 91.4 percent being coal of a higher sulfur content. The low-sulfur coal cost approximately $2.61/ton more than the high-sulfur coal.

6 Motor vehicles fueled with propane gas contribute substantially less air pollutants to the atmosphere than gasoline-fueled vehicles. During 1971 the company converted 9 more of its fleet of 115 vehicles to use of propane gas. The cost of this conversion was $3,700. Seventeen company vehicles are now operated on propane gas.

7 Underground installation of electric transmission lines has increased since environmental attention has focused on the aesthetic pollution of poles and wires. During 1971 the company installed underground electric transmission lines, which cost $737,000 more than putting the same lines above ground.

8 Jackhammers used by the company are, with one exception, of the normal, noise-polluting type. One jackhammer purchased during 1971 with noise controls cost $100 more than the regular jackhammers.

9 The company reimburses employees for educational expenditures and provides recreational opportunities such as the annual company picnic. Such expenditures amounted to approximately $6,000 in 1971.

Source: Dilley and Weygandt, p. 69.

outside agencies (such as university faculties, research centers, or consulting firms) allows for a readily attainable degree of objectivity without requiring the presently impractical standards of a CPA's audit. The disadvantages to the proposal appear to be (*1*) the lack of integration, thus hampering any overall conclusion as to the reporting entity's social performance; (*2*) an intimidating amount of detail, which might be more readily comprehended if summarized in meaningful statistics; (*3*) the requirement for a different set of reports whenever the relevant social concerns and activities differ; and (*4*) the failure to estimate the *value* of social programs and social costs in readily understandable monetary units (dollars), with reporting instead only of dollar outlays.

Corcoran and Leininger's Environmental Exchange Report

One of the earlier responses to the growing concern over the effects of industries on the environment, and one of the most innovative, was advanced by A. Wayne Corcoran and Wayne E. Leininger in 1970.[7] They proposed a report that would reflect all the exchanges between a firm and its environment. This report, reproduced in Exhibit 3-12, would contain sections on the input and output of human resources and physical resources, and would include selected financial data relevant to social concerns. The report is similar to a statement of cash flows that reflects all money exchanges between an entity and the rest of society, but the analogy is not complete. For example, the input of human resources would seem to be the hours of human services diverted by the firm from other activities in society, and this is reported. But the firm can produce no output of human resources (only humans can do that), and thus the output information provided in this category can only be supplemental and explanatory. Further, a complete report on financial exchanges would simply require reproduction of some version of a funds flow statement; Corcoran and Leininger recognize this and seem to assume that the Environmental Exchange Report would be provided along with a flow of funds statement. On the other hand, the analogy with respect to input and output of physical resources appears to be complete—and quite informative.

The Corcoran and Leininger construct would be fairly simple to prepare, although some additional cost would be incurred to routinely provide data on physical quantities. The report would be easy to understand, but it might be difficult to evaluate because of the absence of standards or reference values. A fair degree of comprehensiveness is possible, but certain information pertaining

---

7 A. Wayne Corcoran and Wayne E. Leininger, Jr., "Financial Statements—Who Needs Them?" *Financial Executive,* August 1970, pp. 34–38, 45–47.

EXHIBIT 3-12   XYZ COMPANY. Environmental Exchange Report for Year Ended December 31, 1970

INPUT

Human Resources:

Time—During the year, 100 individuals were hired, bringing total employment to 1,000. Employees made available 2,000,000 man-hours to the firm, and there were no layoffs during the year. 75,000 man-hours were lost because of sickness or other personal reasons, and employees earned 100,000 man-hours of paid vacation.

Time With Firm	Percentage of Employees
under 1 yr.	10
1–3 yrs.	15
3–5 yrs.	42
5–10 yrs.	30
over 10 yrs.	3

Education* Level	Percentage of Employees
under 12 yrs.	20
12 yrs.	40
13–14 yrs.	10
college degree	30

Age of Employees	Percentage of Employees
18 to 25	20
26 to 30	23
31 to 40	27
41 to 50	19
51 to 65	11

* The firm invested $50,000 in assisting employees further their education.

Physical Resources:

Direct Materials—

(A) 500 tons of cast iron (35% of which is recycled scrap metal)

(B) 10,000 tons of steel (30% of which is recycled scrap metal)

The firm pursues a policy of purchasing from manufacturers who not only produce quality products but are also leaders in the area of pollution control.

(C) 200,000 board feet of lumber

The supplier of the lumber estimates that it took 35 years to grow this lumber. This lumber is used in the end product and for packaging and is not recoverable.

77

EXHIBIT 3-12 (Continued)

Indirect Materials—

(A) 500 tons of oil and related products

(B) 5,000,000 gallons of water

(C) 60 tons of paper and related products (20% of which is recycled scrap)

OUTPUT

Human Resources:

10 employees were dismissed, 25 terminated voluntarily, and 13 retired with anual pensions ranging from $3,500 to $10,400 with a mean of $5,200.

Annual Earnings	Mean	Average Increase	Percentage of Employees	Percentage Holding Other Employment	Mean Un-employed Dependents	Mean Years With Firm
under $5,000	$ 4,750	$500	15	75	2.1	2
$5,000–7,499	7,200	600	20	42	4.1	5
$7,500–9,999	8,900	600	40	20	4.3	8
$10,000–14,999	11,700	720	20	5	4.8	11
over $15,000	18,000	840	5	0	3.8	15

Physical Resources:

End Product—500,000 widgets with two-year guarantees, and estimated life of five years. It is thought that the bounty offered for recovery of widgets will result in the return of 75% of the widgets and that 80% of raw materials contained in the recovered widgets will be reprocessed for future use. 100,000 board feet of lumber are not recoverable.

Water—5,000,000 gallons were removed from the Blue River, and 4,000,000 gallons were returned. The installation of several cooling ponds eliminated appreciable thermal pollution to the river. The Massachusetts Department of Natural Resources has certified that the water returned to the river was in all aspects purer than the water removed. The remaining 1,000,000 gallons were dissipated into the atmosphere in the form of steam.

Air—5 tons of solid material in the form of dust were unavoidably emitted into the atmosphere. During the month of June, the firm was fined $3,000 for excessive emissions into the air caused by the breakdown of our air pollution control system. Management decided against suspending production during the breakdown period.

Waste—Packaging of product resulted in 50 tons of paper and plastic waste, and 100,000 board feet of lumber that are not recoverable. 15 tons of solid waste resulted from the production process and are not recoverable in any form.

Financial

	By Firm	By Employees
Taxes Paid		
Federal	$1,000,000	$1,200,000
State	500,000	200,000
Local	450,000	800,000
Contributions		
Colleges and Universities	40,000	20,000
United Fund	10,000	20,000
Massachusetts Social Action Board	10,000	unknown

Source: A. Wayne Corcoran and Wayne E. Leininger, Jr., "Financial Statements—Who Needs Them?" *Financial Executive*, August 1970, pp. 46–47. Used by permission.

to present social concerns (equality of opportunity, social responsibility programs and activities, safety, quality of product) is omitted from the model. The use of several different metrics does not permit calculation of a single net result (although some would argue that this is desirable, since every factor is not forced into a money valuation).

Because of their relative simplicity, low cost, and ready attainability, both the Corcoran and Leininger Environmental Exchange Report and the Dilley and Weygandt Responsibility Annual Report may appeal to firms seeking an immediate avenue to social reporting.

Linowes' Socio-Economic Operating Statement

David Linowes suggests that "social audits" will be required within the next decade for most business organizations, and even disclosure of "Socio-Economic Operating Budgets" for the succeeding year may come to be expected.[8] To meet the growing needs and demands of consumer groups, special institutional investors, and an increasing number of governmental regulatory agencies, Linowes has proposed a periodic Socio-Economic Operating Statement (SEOS—Exhibit 3-13) to accompany an organization's regular financial statements. The SEOS would be prepared by an internal interdisciplinary team headed by an accountant and possibly including a seasoned business executive, sociologist, public health administrator, and economist. Linowes, himself a partner in a large accounting firm, argues that these statements should be audited by an external, independent team headed by a CPA and including representatives of other disciplines as needed.

Linowes' statement would report detriments netted against improvements in each of three categories: relations with people, relations with environment, and relations with product. The result is added to past cumulative socioeconomic improvements. "Improvements" in the statement reflect the money cost of expenditures made *voluntarily* to improve the welfare of employees and the public, to enhance safety of the product, or to protect or improve the environment. Any expenditures that are required, such as by law or union contract, would not be reported.

"Detriments" reflect the *cost avoided* or not incurred for needed actions that are brought to management's attention by a "responsible authority," so long as the need is "of such a nature that a *reasonably prudent and socially aware*

8 David F. Linowes, "An Approach to Socio-Economic Accounting," *Conference Board RECORD,* November 1972, pp. 58–61.

business management would have responded favorably.[9] Examples of improvements and detriments are given in Exhibit 3-13.

Of the social reporting proposals considered so far, Linowes' Socio-Economic Operating Statement is the first to call for full use of money values in an integrated, matching mode that produces a single net result. Such a net result is important to effectively communicate, in understandable and comparable terms, information as to the *total* social performance of the reporting entity. Linowes notes the dilemma of the socially responsible company that, by incurring expenditures not incurred by less socially responsible competitors, is "penalized" on its profit and loss statement. By undertaking to match social improvements against social detriments, Linowes has provided a vehicle in which the socially responsible company looks better on the "bottom line"—a result that is both fairer and socially desirable.

All the proposals discussed in this chapter involve subjectivity to some degree, as do traditional financial statements; but the definition of detriments in Linowes' statement calls for a degree of subjectivity that could destroy the usefulness of the report. Furthermore, measurement of detriments as the cost avoided may disguise the *real* cost to society. (Studies have suggested that the ratio between damage to society and abatement or prevention costs may be as great as 16:1.)

Linowes has advanced a model that is commendable in comprehensiveness, format, and the use of money values—but its allowance of untenable subjectivity and a tendency to report the *wrong* cost limit its usefulness for external social reporting.

Abt's Social Audit

Clark Abt, president of the consulting firm of Abt Associates, Inc., has noted that companies which are quite careful and analytical with respect to their "business" investments often manage their "social" investments on an arbitrary and sentimental basis; he thus argues that there is "a great need to apply rational management techniques to the task of increasing social return on corporate investment."[10] To this end, Abt advocates a "social audit." Abt's approach to a social audit is presented in Exhibit 2-4. (In Chapter 2 the Abt

---

9 *Ibid.*, p. 59.
10 Clark Abt, "Managing to Save Money While Doing Good," *Innovation*, No. 27, 1972, pp. 38–47.

EXHIBIT 3-13 XXXX Corporation

Socio-Economic Operating Statement for the Year Ending December 31, 1971

I *Relations with People:*

A. *Improvements:*

   1. Training program for handi-capped workers ... $ 10,000

   2. Contribution to edu-cational institution ... 4,000

   3. Extra turnover costs be-cause of minority hiring program ... 5,000

   4. Cost of nursery school for children of employees, voluntarily set up ... 11,000

   Total Improvements ... $ 30,000

B. *Less: Detriments*

   1. Postponed installing new safety devices on cutting machines (cost of the de-vices) ... 14,000

C. Net Improvements in People Actions for the Year ... $ 16,000

II *Relations with Environment:*

A. *Improvements:*

B. *Less: Detriments*

   1. Cost that would have been incurred to relandscape strip mining site used this year ... $ 80,000

   2. Estimated costs to have in-stalled purification process to neutralize poisonous liquid being dumped into stream ... $100,000 ... $180,000

C. Net Deficit in Environment Actions for the Year ... ($ 97,000)

III *Relations with Product:*

A. *Improvements:*

   1. Salary of V.P. while serving on government Product Safety Commission ... $ 25,000

   2. Cost of substituting lead-free paint for previously used poisonous lead paint ... 9,000

   Total Improvements ... $ 34,000

II Relations with Environment:
  A. Improvements:
    1. Cost of reclaiming and
        landscaping old dump on
        company property $ 70,000
    2. Cost of installing pollu-
        tion control devices on
        Plant A smokestacks   4,000
    3. Cost of detoxifying waste
        from finishing process
        this year   9,000
                                                 _____
        Total Improvements $ 83,000

  B. Less: Detriments
    1. Safety device recommended
        by Safety Council but not
        added to product $ 22,000
                                                          _____

  C. Net Improvements in Product
      Actions for the Year $ 12,000
                                                          _____

      Total Socio-Economic Deficit for the Year   ($ 69,000)

      Add: Net Cumulative Socio-Economic
           Improvements as at January 1, 1971 $249,000
                                                         _____

      GRAND TOTAL NET SOCIO-ECONOMIC
      ACTIONS TO DECEMBER 31, 1971 $180,000
                                                         ========

Source: David F. Linowes, "An Approach to Socio-Economic Accounting," *Conference Board RECORD*, November 1972, p. 60. © The Conference Board. Used by permission.

83

report is discussed as a case of social accounting; here we are interested in the report as a *model* or proposal for social reporting.)

The Abt model presents both stocks (balance sheet) and flows (income statement). All measurements are in money units, as contrasted to physical quantities, rates of change, or other units of measure. The 1974 report/model attempts to integrate both traditional financial and social effects into a single set of statements (although this attempt at integration, while commendable, is nevertheless difficult to follow). The model provides for extensive explanatory footnotes to explain concepts and measurement approaches; such detailed explanations are appropriate in any reporting model during the present evolutionary stage of social accounting.

The earlier Abt social accounting models took society's viewpoint. That is, all effects were reported from society's point of view rather than from that of the entity. The current model, used for the 1974 report, is ambiguous in this regard, since some of the data are derived strictly from the entity's viewpoint (financial effects, for example) while other effects appear to reflect society's (such as environmental resources used through pollution). This criticism may not be entirely deserved, since the confusion may be more in the eyes of this beholder than in the model; but it is nevertheless difficult to see clearly just what viewpoint was intended for the social audit taken as a whole.

The model includes a form of human resource accounting. The present value of the staff is capitalized as a social asset, as is the training investment net of amortization for training obsolescence. The benefit to staff from career advancement, and costs of layoffs, involuntary terminations, and inequality of opportunity, are also estimated.

Most current proposals for social accounting for profit-seeking entities ignore the basic economic or operational mission of the firm. In its 1971 report, Abt experimented with this sort of information by including a separate section that was placed at the bottom of the Social Income Statement but not added into the statement totals. This section reported "Social Benefits to Clients" of $22,337,500 for 1971, explained as follows:

> Benefits to clients from contract work completed are computed by adding multiplier effects expressible in dollar equivalent terms to contract revenues, and subtracting contract revenues of work not used by the client (and thus offering him no benefit). Multiplier effects include savings developed for clients by contracts beyond the value of the contracts, and resources mobilized for the client as a direct result of the contract and beyond its value. If there is no desirable multiplier impact of the work, but it is used by the client as in-

formation, it is assumed to be worth merely what was paid for it. An alternate assumption is that multiplier effects accrue in an as yet indeterminate way, and that therefore they should not be used to add to benefits. Under this assumption, contract work for clients is worth what is paid for it, and no more and no less.[11]

Costs to clients of contract work completed, labeled "Social Costs to Clients," amounted to $4,572,459; the excess of estimated benefits to clients over costs was thus $17,765,041. Although it is easy to criticize any estimate of the value of services rendered or products sold that exceeds the amount actually paid in arms-length exchange transactions, we must nevertheless recognize that "consumers' surplus" and bargain purchases do occur, probably much more frequently than commercial fraud or overpricing. (Consumers' surplus is considered more thoroughly in Chapter 5.) Abt omitted this information from its 1972 report, noting that "research is still underway to more rigorously quantify these benefits." In 1973 and 1974 direct benefits to clients were reported as contract cost plus staff overtime worked but not paid for, offset by cost of contracts to clients. It seems reasonable to estimate the benefit to clients of unbilled overtime, but this approach is still unlikely to capture the full value of consumers' surplus. Abt is once again on the right track in its 1974 model, and should continue with its efforts to estimate and report the full value of work done for clients.

The Abt model appears to make no distinction between direct effects and indirect effects. For example, social liabilities are recognized for pollution generated by suppliers of electricity and paper; Abt does make an *indirect* contribution to this pollution by using these products, but the pollution is created directly by the utility and paper manufacturing companies.

The treatment of pollution costs also raises a question about the articulation of the income statement and the balance sheet. As noted in Chapter 2, the net social incomes "are assumed to be distributed as they are created; they do not flow into the social balance sheet since such social earnings are not retained." This seems to be Abt's explanation for the lack of articulation between the two statements. But social costs of pollution are simply added to previous liability balances to produce ending liability balances. It is difficult to conceive how these liabilities will ever be liquidated. More important, consistent logic would require that all noninternalized externalities be internalized in a like manner;

---

11 Abt Associates, Inc., *1971 Annual Report + Social Audit* (Cambridge, Mass., 1971), p. 31.

external economies (social benefits) would directly increase social assets or decrease social liabilities, and external diseconomies would have the opposite effect.

To summarize, the Abt "social audit" model is commendably ambitous. It seeks to present stocks as well as flows, and it has been used on a real if unrepresentative company (Abt Associates is a service and consulting organization that neither manufactures nor sells a tangible product, possibly excepting publications). The model reflects a high degree of quantification of information, and all quantities are ultimately valued in money terms. Negative as well as positive effects are included and matched against each other to produce a net or "bottom line" result. However, some parts of the reports are still difficult to understand and are not adequately explained.

For the company developing its own social accounting techniques, the Abt model warrants serious study. The Social and Financial Balance Sheet may prove to be useful for internal purposes, but appears to provide little in the way of useful information for the public. The Social and Financial Income Statement can serve as a useful basis for developing a public report, although significant modifications will be required for different industries. The measurement approaches and bases for estimates, which are described in the footnotes, should be particularly useful in suggesting ways of quantifying various social effects.

Seidler's Social Income Statement

Lee Seidler has sketched a social reporting approach that, though lacking in detail, is conceptually the most advanced of those discussed in this chapter.[12] He suggests two social income statement formats, one for a profit-seeking organization (Exhibit 3-14) and another for a not-for-profit organization using a university as an example (Exhibit 3-15); these formats, while deceptively simple, are capable of accepting *all* the effects of an entity on society.

In addition to reflecting the contribution of a profit-seeking entity from its basic economic activity (approximated by the revenues and costs reported in the traditional income statement), the social income statement adds socially desirable outputs for which no money is received (external economies) and deducts costs that the entity imposes on society but does not pay for (external diseconomies). The result is a net social profit or loss reflecting the net contribution of the entity to society.

12 Lee J. Seidler, "Dollar Values in the Social Income Statement," *World* (Peat Marwick Mitchell & Co.), Spring 1973, pp. 14, 16–23.

EXHIBIT 3-14   **Social Income Statement for a Profit-Seeking Organization**

Value added by production of the enterprise		$xxx
Add socially desirable outputs not sold		
Job training	$xxx	
Health improvement of workers	xxx	
Employment of disadvantaged minorities	xxx	
Other	xxx	xxx
		$xxx
Less socially undesirable effects not paid for		
Air pollution	$xxx	
Water pollution	xxx	
Health problems caused by products	xxx	
Other	xxx	xxx
Net social profit (or loss)		$xxx

Source: Adapted with minor modifications from Lee J. Seidler, "Dollar Values in the Social Income Statement," *World* (Peat Marwick Mitchell & Co.), Spring 1973, p. 21.

Because of the difficulty of estimating value added for an institution, such as a university, in which payments for services rendered do not come exclusively from the beneficiaries of those services (but also from grants, legislative appropriations, and the like), the social income statement for many not-for-profit organizations would simply have two sections: one for benefits to society (unfortunately labeled "revenues" by Seidler) and another for costs to society. As in the statement for profit-seeking organizations, this format allows for recognition of benefits and costs that are not formalized through market transactions, such as contributions to knowledge or air pollution.

Seidler notes the difficulty in assigning money values to all items in his statements; but he argues that money measurements are the most common language of most people and are thus most useful in social accounting, even though some items may be expressed as simple ordinal measures (rankings) as an intermediate step.

Of the two models proposed by Seidler, the one for not-for-profit organizations is more informative because it provides estimates of total social benefits and total social costs, rather than netting many important effects, as does the value added approach. Both formats are comprehensive—they allow for report-

EXHIBIT 3-15   Social Income Statement for a University

Revenues		
Value of instruction to society		$xxx
Value of research to society		xxx
Total revenues		$xxx
Less costs		
Tuition paid to university	$xxx	
Cost of research	xxx	
State aid	xxx	
Others—lost production, etc.	xxx	
Total costs		xxx
Profit to society		$xxx

Source: Adapted with minor modifications from Lee J. Seidler, "Dollar Values in the Social Income Statement," *World* (Peat Marwick Mitchell & Co.), Spring 1973, p. 18.

ing *all* significant effects of an entity on society—and both are flexible enough to accommodate changing social concerns. While lacking sufficient detail to serve as a complete guide, the Seidler proposal provides a generally sound conceptual framework for social reporting.

SUMMARY

Since a proposal for an "environmental exchange report" was advanced by Corcoran and Leininger in 1970, a number of social accounting models have been developed. This chapter discusses the most important proposals. As the following listing shows, they range from the simple to the highly complex:

1. Narrative disclosure, in footnotes to financial statements, of information concerning environmental problems and efforts (AAA).
2. Extension of traditional financial statements to include certain accounts related to environmental matters (Beams; AAA).
3. Nonmonetary information on pollution-control facilities and emissions (Marlin).
4. Several schedules covering pollution, occupational health and safety, and

equal employment opportunity information; nonmonetary except for a schedule of outlays in these areas (Dilley and Weygandt).

5. A report of inputs and outputs, both human and physical, as well as amounts of taxes paid and contributions (Corcoran and Leininger).

6. Information on voluntary expenditures made for the welfare of employees and the public, offset by the avoided cost of socially desirable actions not taken (Linowes).

7. A complex "social audit" with sections dealing with the company and stock-holders, employees, clients and the general public, and the community; all amounts monetized (Abt).

8. A comprehensive report of all benefits and costs to society resulting from an entity's activities, with money measures recommended (Seidler).

All of these proposals are reasonably practical; that is, they are "doable" within a range of difficulty, reliability, and cost. Three have been tried on actual companies: data suggested in Marlin's reports were externally gathered on paper companies by the Council on Economic Priorities; Dilley and Weygandt tested their model on an unidentified Midwestern gas and electric utility company; and Abt Associates first published their social reports in their 1971 annual report. Information for the Dilley and Weygandt report should be readily available in reports already required by government agencies and elsewhere within a company; the AAA, Beams, and Marlin proposals require new information that should be easily developed within a firm; amounts for the Linowes report could be readily obtained, but deciding which items to report would be difficult because of the subjectivity involved; the Abt and Seidler models would require unusual effort and some difficult measurements (but note that these problems have not prevented Abt Associates from producing its reports).

What is the potential usefulness of these models? Internally, the most complex models should be the most useful—for even if management were unable or unwilling to commit the resources necessary to develop *all* the information, it should still learn about what is going on within the company and where the potential trouble spots are (and the potential assessments, lawsuits, or other liabilities).

Externally, all the models should be useful, but in varying degrees. The Seidler, Abt, Corcoran and Leininger, and Dilley and Weygandt reports are the most complete. The most understandable approaches should be Dilley and Weygandt, the AAA narrative disclosure, Marlin, Corcoran and Leininger, and Seidler, in that order. In terms of reliability, the AAA and Beams extensions to financial reports would be covered by the independent auditor's opinion, while several of the Dilley and Weygandt schedules could be checked against reports filed with the government. For many purposes a single number measure is desirable; only the Seidler, Abt, and Linowes models produce such a net or bottom line result.

Each of the models discussed in this chapter has something to commend it, but none is both comprehensive and fully developed. In Chapter 4 we develop a comprehensive model for reporting the total direct impact of an organization.

*When we mean to build, we first survey the
plot, then draw the model.*

Shakespeare, King Henry IV

4 A Comprehensive Social Accounting Model

Should American taxpayers have been called on to help bail out Lockheed Air-craft and Penn Central? It was argued that both provide essential benefits to the nation, but are these benefits great enough to justify the drastic actions that were taken? In other words, are the benefits provided by these companies to the nation expected to exceed the costs to society of ensuring their survival? Un-fortunately, the information required to answer this question was not available at the time Congress acted and is not available now.

We do know something about the products and services provided by a firm, and we can see the reported revenue, which supposedly reflects the best price the seller could get (he would accept more) and the lowest price the buyer could find (but would he pay more?). What we don't know is the magnitude of "consumers' surplus" resulting from bargain purchases, or "consumers' deficit" resulting from fraud, misleading advertising, or unsafe products. And while we are told about the costs that the company has to pay for, what about the damage it causes that it *doesn't* pay for—pollution, noise, discrimination, fraud, bribery?

To resolve issues such as those involved in the Lockheed and Penn Central cases intelligently, to decide on legislation that would prevent air pollution but might also put some firms out of business, and to use our scarce resources wisely and efficiently, we need to know the net direct contribution of each entity to society—whether this entity provides benefits to society greater than the costs imposed, or vice versa. We need an accounting model that systematically reflects the worth of all resources consumed, including those resources or values which are free to the consuming entity (noninternalized costs or external diseconomies), and the worth of all benefits produced, includ-ing those that provide no compensation to the producing entity (external economies). Such a model is proposed in this chapter.

The meanings of several terms used in this chapter should be clarified at this point.

- *Society:* all elements of the environment external to the reporting entity, including other companies, the populace, and even single individuals.
- *Value:* quantified worth or utility. The value of any resource depends on the existence of some social welfare function; no particular function is specified or assumed in this book, but it is recognized that measurement of any benefit or cost partially reflects such a function.
- *Social resource:* anything—tangible or intangible—having a net positive value to society. Thus clean air is a resource, as are minerals, land, highways, clean waterways, human services, and beauty. Even though it lacks intrinsic value, money is treated as a resource when transfers between the reporting entity and the rest of society are considered.
- *Social benefit:* any benefit to society (or to any element of society), whether economic or "noneconomic," internal or external. Thus social benefits include those benefits provided by an entity for which it is compensated as well as those "external economies" and bargains for which no compensation (or inadequate compensation) is received.
- *Social cost:* any cost, sacrifice, or detriment to society (or to any element of society), whether economic or noneconomic, internal or external. Social costs include sacrifices for which compensation is made (such as human services used and paid for) as well as detriments not paid for (such as air pollution); any payments are treated separately as a benefit to society. (Traditionally the term *social cost* has been used to refer only to consumption or damage to society with no associated pecuniary cost to the offending or consuming entity, and thus not internalized by it, i.e., external diseconomies; the reader should be careful to note the broader, more inclusive meaning assigned here.)

A COMPREHENSIVE SOCIAL BENEFIT/COST MODEL

Complex economic systems rely on specialization among entities to increase output; users do not attempt to produce all their needs. Resources are allocated—or find their way—to producers who are expected to return benefits with values at least equal to, but hopefully in excess of, the values of the resources used. The allocation process is sometimes quite formal (federal research grants, for example), usually rather informal (the price/market system), and in some cases completely unstructured (comsumption of clean air, silence, and highways).

Maximization of net social benefits (taking some unspecified social welfare function as given) requires effective allocations that depend on reasonably complete and valid information. To reflect the full effect of the entity on society, this information should at least include identification of, and preferably a valuation for, each significant social benefit provided and social cost incurred by an entity. Allocations at present depend heavily on information provided through the financial accounting model, which excludes certain benefits (external economies) and detriments (external diseconomies). The financial accounting model generally reflects the view of the entity looking out, toward society; benefits (products and services) provided to society are thus indicated by the surrogate of revenues received, whereas costs are measured only by the entity's expenditures.[1] Improved resource allocations could result from a different viewpoint, that of society looking toward the entity. Benefits to society would then be measured by the values or utilities actually received by society (which may differ from the amount paid to the entity); while costs would reflect the full detriments to society, and not only those for which the entity pays. These opposing viewpoints are illustrated in Exhibit 4-1.

To provide the information required for rational resource allocation, a model

EXHIBIT 4-1   Reporting Viewpoints

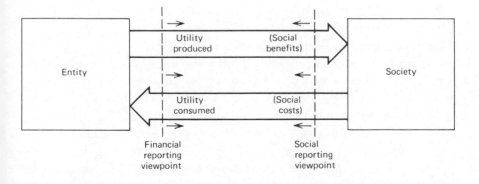

---

1 All significant costs presently reported are measured by expenditures, although the expenditures may not occur in the period in which the related costs are reported. This difference, of course, leads to accruals, amortizations, and allocations.

having the following structure is proposed:

$$SS = \sum_{i=1}^{n} \sum_{t=1}^{\infty} \frac{B_i}{(1 + r)^t} - \sum_{j=1}^{m} \sum_{t=i}^{\infty} \frac{C_j}{(1 + r)^t}$$

where SS = social surplus or deficit,

B_i = the ith social benefit,

C_j = the jth social cost,

r = an appropriate discount rate,

t = time period in which benefit or cost is expected to occur.

A comprehensive social report based on this model is presented in Exhibit 4-2.

Care must be taken in defining the reporting entity or system. The corporation or other organization, as legally constituted and publicly recognized, is the starting point. Included are all activities of employees carried on in behalf of the entity and while "on-duty." Activities of a board of directors and of stockholders acting collectively for the entity are included. Excluded from the system for reporting purposes are personal activities of employees, including commuting; activity of customers, including use or misuse of the product; and all other secondary or indirect effects.

This point should perhaps be amplified. The proposed model is a comprehensive report of the direct effects of a single entity on society. It is not designed to show what would happen (how society would be better or worse off) if the entity had not existed during the reporting period; this would require the reporting of such indirect effects as a pro rata share of pollution caused by suppliers and detriments produced by users of the entity's products. A model including such information would certainly be useful but would involve substantial double-counting among entities.

The present model could in fact reflect indirect effects, but only if they were internalized (i.e., built into the entity's cost and rewards structure). This would occur if (*a*) *each* element of society accurately measured and reported all social benefits and costs created, (*b*) each element were periodically assessed or rewarded an amount equal to its net social surplus or deficit, and (*c*) each element then adjusted the prices of its goods and services upward in response to assessments or downward for rewards. Of course these conditions do not presently obtain; consequently the proposed model reflects significant indirect effects only in footnotes.

The report should be prepared for the entire entity, i.e., it should be "consolidated." In addition, whenever possible, reports should be prepared for each community in which a component of the entity operates, reflecting the social impact on that community alone. Local government bodies, citizens, and other concerned elements of a community need to know the effects of a corporate division on their community; they are less interested in, and have less need for, information regarding the corporation's national or world impact.

All significant costs and benefits are reported "gross"; netting is avoided. For example, the cost to society of human services used by the reporting entity and the benefit to society in compensation paid might logically be netted against each other, but in the proposed report each would be separately disclosed. This approach permits the disclosure of *total* benefits and *total* costs—useful information for evaluating the total impact of the organization on society. It also focuses attention on value separate from exchange price; the latter may disguise bargain purchases, fraud, lack of information, and various market aberrations. The report may thus appear to count the same item twice, but this appearance is deceptive, because it results from the presentation of both sides of each activity or transaction.

All items in the report are valued in dollars. This may be disturbing for two reasons: dollar values (*1*) are more difficult to estimate than other quantities and (*2*) are perceived by some as antihuman (suggesting "pursuit of the almighty dollar"). But it must be recognized that dollars are only a neutral means of *weighting* other quantities to obtain homogeneous numbers that can be compared and added. Other weights, such as "utils," "plaisirs" (as Lee Seidler has suggested), or even "vals," could be used, but we are accustomed to thinking of values in terms of dollars and the economic system already provides us with estimates in dollars of several of the items in the model.

It should be emphasized that this model is somewhat idealistic and may not be presently practical for all firms; the objective here is to suggest a standard, a goal, for social reporting. Nevertheless, much of the information is already available in every corporation, and a serious effort should produce adequate estimates for completion of the report in most companies.

The components of the model are now discussed in some detail.

Social Benefits

Products and Services Provided.   Corporations generally exist to provide products and services; these are purchased by customers, which provides *prima facie* evidence of benefit to society. The starting point for valuing such benefits is the exchange prices usually arrived at in response to demand and supply factors. In other words, an automobile that sells for $4000 presumably is expected

EXHIBIT 4-2
The Progressive Company
Social Impact Statement For the Year Ended December 31, 19x1

Social Benefits			
Products and services provided		$xxx	
Payments to other elements of society			
Employment provided (salaries and wages)	$xxx		
Payments for goods and other services	xxx		
Taxes paid	xxx		
Contributions	xxx		
Dividends and interest paid	xxx		
Loans and other payments	xxx	xxx	
Additional direct employee benefits		xxx	
Staff, equipment, and facility services donated		xxx	
Environmental improvements		xxx	
Other benefits		xxx	
Total Social Benefits			$xxx
Social Costs			
Goods and materials acquired		$xxx	
Buildings and equipment purchased		xxx	
Labor and services used		xxx	
Discrimination			
In hiring (external)	$xxx		
In placement and promotion (internal)	xxx	xxx	
Work-related injuries and illness		xxx	
Public services and facilities used		xxx	
Other resources used		xxx	
Environmental damage			
Terrain damage	$xxx		
Air pollution	xxx		
Water pollution	xxx		
Noise pollution	xxx		
Solid waste	xxx		
Visual and aesthetic pollution	xxx		
Other environmental damage	xxx	xxx	
Payments from other elements of society			
Payments for goods and services provided	$xxx		
Additional capital investment	xxx		
Loans	xxx		
Other payments received	xxx	xxx	
Other costs		xxx	
Total Social Costs			xxx
Social Surplus (Deficit) for the Year			$xxx
Accumulated Surplus (Deficit) December 31, 19x0			xxx
Accumulated Surplus (Deficit) December 31, 19x1			$xxx

EXHIBIT 4-2 (Continued)

Standard Footnotes
1. Significant indirect effects associated with inputs.
2. Significant indirect effects associated with outputs.
3. Bases for measurements and estimates.
4. Progress in areas of current societal concern (such as environmental protection outlays and activities, employment and promotion of minorities and women, and energy conservation efforts).

to provide to the purchaser, one element of society, benefits having a present value of at least $4000.

Included in this category of benefits are facilities, equipment, and space provided to other elements of society, for which rent is received.

Upward adjustments, reflecting "consumers' surplus," are required when exchange prices do not adequately measure benefits. Care must be exercised, however, to value only direct effects from the products and services provided. Suppose that the automobile referred to above provided the purchaser utility having an estimated present value of $4200, and that he in turn used the auto to provide free transportation to and from work for several neighbors, resulting in additional benefits to the neighbors (but not to the owner) estimated at $500. The amount to be reported by the selling corporation, including $200 in consumer surplus, would be $4200, not $4000 or $4700 (the automobile owner could report social benefits provided of $500). Significant indirect effects should be reported in footnotes, but not integrated into the model, since they are not actually provided by the reporting entity.

Downward adjustments are required when the exchange price exceeds the utility provided (indicating "consumers' deficit"). This can occur when purchasers have inadequate information, when products are dangerous or unsafe, when benefits are exaggerated through false advertising and promotion, or when threats and extortion occur.

It is tempting to argue that downward adjustments should be made for products that pollute or in other ways are detrimental to society. The responsibility for such detriments rests primarily on the *user*, not the producer, and double-counting would result if both the user and the producer were charged with these detriments. Air pollution caused by automobiles is a good example of this problem. Producers can be induced (or required) to develop low pollution-generating automobiles, but users sometimes disconnect the control devices—or they simply fail to maintain them properly. If automobile users were assessed (perhaps by using sealed odometers and annual inspections in conjunction with license renewal) for pollution generated, users would then have an incentive to (*1*) purchase automobiles with efficient pollution-control devices, (*2*) maintain such devices in good working order, and (*3*) drive fewer miles, thus generating less pollution.[2]

Any benefits to be realized in future periods should be discounted to present values; the same is true, of course, for costs.

Payments to Other Elements of Society.   We usually think of raw material consumption as a cost or detriment to society, and indeed it is—but when such materials are paid for by the user, benefits are provided commensurate with the amount of payment. Thus corporations render benefits to various elements of society as they pay for goods and services used.

The value of employment provided should be separately disclosed; that is, payments to employees represent a social benefit in the amount of money transmitted to such employees and made available for their use. Since the value of human services used is separately reported as a social cost, compensation that is less than the value of services used results in a lower net social surplus (or greater social deficit).

Other significant payments included in this section include loans, contributions, dividends, interest, taxes, and assessments. It should be noted that the benefit provided by a corporation disbursing money is the money itself; what the recipient entity does with that money should be credited to that separate entity. This is especially important for charitable contributions. Here again, significant indirect effects might be reported in a footnote but should not be integrated into the model.

Inclusion of payments to society as a benefit (and, later in the discussion, including payments received from society as a cost) may appear to involve double-counting or at least confounding of values. This construction may be better understood if we consider that the typical operation involves goods and services

---

2 Solid waste is a more difficult question than air or noise pollution. Cost of disposal, processing, or recycling is primarily a function of design, and the purchaser has limited choice in this regard. He can, of course, seek to buy beer in returnable bottles, cereal in biodegradable packages, and automobiles with longer expected lives, but his choices in such respects are generally quite limited, and in some cases nonexistent. Disposal costs should probably still be charged to users for *reporting* purposes, but society may then elect to assess or tax producers. A distinction must be made between proper reporting in terms of direct responsibility (the objective of the proposed model) and normative solutions to social problems (which must reflect political considerations).

provided by elements of society to the firm (a social cost) for which the firm makes payment (a social benefit); by reporting the cost and the benefit separately, the model recognizes that they may not always be equal and, in fact, forces separate measurement. The firm then sells the finished product (and provides a social benefit to the recipients) and receives payment in return (a social cost); again, the benefit and the cost may not be equal. This means that, if the firm were to pay an amount exactly equal to the sacrifices made by the providers of goods and services, and were also to collect an amount exactly equal to the benefits provided through the sale of products, no net social benefit or cost would result. This seems to contradict the general notion that firms provide "value added" through their manufacturing and operating processes. The key is in the viewpoint taken in the model—that of society viewing the firm, rather than the firm viewing its own operations. In the latter case, value added does indeed result, as profits; in the former, only equal exchanges occur under the conditions described (of course if these conditions always obtained, the proposed model would be useless).

Additional Direct Employee Benefits. The value of most fringe benefits should be reported in this category. So should the value of experience provided, training programs, special opportunities provided, and rewarding work that provides utility to the employee over and above the monetary remuneration.

This category involves unusual measurement problems. What is the value to participants of a company-sponsored bowling league, a company cafeteria, executive washrooms, training programs? The proper valuation is the utility provided to employees, *not* the cost to the company (which is reflected separately as an outlay). Employee surveys and shadow pricing should be helpful in estimating these values.

Staff, Equipment, and Facility Services Donated. When corporations loan officers and employees to charitable, social, and other community organizations, benefits are provided separate from the compensation paid to the employees. These benefits might be estimated at the cost that would have been incurred by the outside organization if it had hired persons with the qualifications required. Such required qualifications may be less than the qualifications actually possessed by employees on loan, in which case the value of the benefits provided to the outside organization is less than the compensation paid by the reporting entity.

Only services performed on behalf of the reporting entity or in the role of its employee should be credited to it. Purely individual and personal activities should be credited to the individual, not to the firm. The problem thus created may often be difficult but should not be insurmountable; in two previous applications of the model only minor difficulty was encountered in distinguishing between company and personal activities. For example, it was clear that work with the United Fund, Chamber of Commerce, National Alliance of Businessmen, and professional organizations was all company; while church and political activities were personal (we were perhaps fortunate in not encountering any illegal political activities in behalf of the firm).

Corporations sometimes allow community groups to use otherwise idle equipment and facilities. Benefits may thus be provided even though there is virtually no cost to the corporation. The value of these benefits may be estimated as the amount of rent the user organizations would have paid if they had rented other facilities. This may be different from, and probably less than, the amount of rent the corporation could have obtained for the facilities if it had rented them to a profit-making organization.

Environmental Improvements.   When corporations restore previously strip-mined areas, plant trees, landscape eroded terrain, and clean polluted lakes, benefits accrue to society. The corporation is charged for the social costs of environmental damage done; hence it should receive credit for benefits provided through restoration of a previously damaged environment. Valuation is difficult for these benefits and is probably *not* accurately reflected by the amount of outlay. Community surveys, shadow pricing, and economic studies might be used to develop suitable estimates.

Other Benefits.   Corporations may provide to society benefits not falling within the above classes. These would include such programs as free day-care centers, special assistance to minority enterprises (other than donated staff services), and sponsorship of public-interest television programs at a cost exceeding the advertising value.

Social Costs

Goods and Materials Acquired.   Raw materials acquired by an entity represent a sacrifice to society to the extent of the value in alternative use. Some raw materials are fixed in supply and cannot be replaced or regenerated for eons (fossil fuels, for example); others can be replaced over several years or perhaps a generation (hardwood trees); still other resources can be regenerated in as little as a year (such as food crops). Feasibility of replacement is a major consideration in valuation of such materials; so is the substitutability of other resources. For example, solar energy may eventually become cheaply available, and may thus devalue fossil fuels.

These factors only suggest the difficulty of measuring the sacrifice or cost to society of the consumption of raw materials. An operational approach might be to value materials with short replacement cycles at their exchange prices minus estimated producers' surplus, while adjusting the value of those with longer cycles to reflect world supply and long-term prospects for development of substitutes.

Building and Equipment Purchases.   When the reporting entity acquires a building or piece of equipment, the utility from that item is lost to the rest of society for as long as it is held by the entity. This cost to society should be approximated by the exchange price, adjusted downward for producers' surplus.

Note that in this approach there is no cost to society as the capital assets are used by their owner. The full cost occurs at the moment of transfer from the rest of society to the reporting entity, and is measured by the discounted present value of the future stream of benefits that the seller would have received had they not been sacrificed in the exchange.

Note also that, as with other social costs, benefits from use of long-term assets are returned to society as goods and services.

Labor and Services Used.   The cost to society of human services used is the sacrifice in time and effort made by the employees (as elements of society); this can probably be approximated by the benefits that they could obtain in alternative employment and other activities. This raises difficult measurement questions. What would be the most valuable alternative service? What would its value be? Would the employee be working at all if not employed by the reporting entity? Furthermore, the answers to these questions vary with the level of unemployment, technological developments, and cultural changes such as reverence for the work ethic. When these measurements involve excessive subjectivity, however, it may be reasonable to simply value employee services at the amount paid for them, with some adjustment for underemployment and underutilization, nepotism, favoritism, producers' surplus, and the like.

Discrimination.   Entities may engage in two forms of discrimination: external discrimination, or discrimination in hiring, and internal discrimination, or discrimination in placement, advancement, and training. External discrimination imposes direct costs on those women and minorities (or any other targets of discrimination, for that matter) who would otherwise have been hired by the company. Their social cost is the present value of income lost and the value of experience foregone. One study places the amount of lost income from racial discrimination at 13% of present white incomes.[3]

The social cost of internal discrimination is the present value of lifetime sacrificed income and experience caused by a delay in advancement of one year (continuing discrimination in succeeding years would be charged in the social reports of those years). Internal discrimination should be easier to value, since a limited number of specifically identifiable individuals are involved. Of course efforts to trace and value either form of discrimination are hampered by the reluctance of managers to admit that it exists, especially in *their* departments.

Work-Related Injuries and Illness.   Any injuries and illnesses attributed to the entity and its activities should be reported as a social cost. This cost can of course be reduced by installation of safety devices, elimination of unhealthy conditions, health monitoring, and similar efforts.

The cost of an injury or illness might be estimated as the present value of lost income plus an increment for pain and discomfort, frustration, and delayed experience. While some will balk at such an apparently crass approach, especially when death is involved, failure to make a serious attempt at cost estimation may result in only personal and emotional impressions, which may play down or magnify the loss. Absence of a cost estimate may in fact lead to an implicit valuation of zero.

Public Services and Facilities Used.   This category includes the reporting entity's share of police and fire protection, the legislative and judicial systems, and government activities at all levels. Many of these services are so pervasive as to make estimation of one entity's share exceptionally difficult. The amount of taxes paid might be used as a starting point, but this amount should be adjusted for unusual costs caused by unsafe plants, inadequately secured assets, exceptionally high-valued merchandise, and so forth. In addition, industry studies might be under-taken to produce guidelines or adjustment factors for firms within the industry.

If material, the cost of public facilities used should be separately disclosed. This category would include damage done to streets, highways, bridges, parks, public buildings, and the like.

Estimation of the relevant cost of public services and facilities used presents

---

3 G. Becker, *Economics of Discrimination* (University of Chicago Press, 1957), pp. 22–23.

perhaps the greatest measurement problem encountered with this model. Imagination and research will produce a variety of techniques, some clever and some unrealistic. Reporting entities may have little feasible choice but to use the amount of taxes paid, adjusted as suggested above, as a surrogate for these two costs—at least until better and more realistic measures are developed.

Other Resources Used.   This category includes not only other purchased materials, such as office and manufacturing supplies, components, and parts, but also utility contained in unpurchased goods and materials that the corporation may consume. These may include donated goods, certain "public" goods (such as those taken from the oceans), stolen goods, and those accidentally or even purposely destroyed for which payment is not made.

Environmental Damage.   The entity imposes damage on the evironment most noticeably through the production and waste disposal processes, but damage is also done by delivery trucks, salesmen's automobiles, construction, and some advertising. The damage comes in several forms: air and water pollution, noise, plant-life destruction, terrain damage (and drainage modification), trash and litter, and even visual pollution. (Solid waste damages the environment when it is disposed of in open dumps; when solid waste is recycled, incinerated, used in landfills, or otherwise processed by government agencies, the social cost is recognized under the "public services used" and "public facilities used" categories.)

In measuring environmental damage, the objective is to estimate the utility lost to society through the entity's activities or omissions. In the case of water pollution, estimates may be sought for lost recreational utility, value of fish and plant life destroyed, increased treatment cost downstream, and impairment of living conditions proximate to the waterway. Air pollution may require estimates of lost utility due to pollution-related illnesses (medical costs, lost productivity, shortened life span, and pain and discomfort), damage to exterior finishes, impairment of living conditions, and plant life damaged or destroyed. The social cost of noise may be based on estimates of the value of current discomfort and long-term hearing impairment. Terrain damage may be estimated as the lesser of two quantities: the value of lost utility (including some value for landscape attractiveness) and the cost of restoration to an original, unimpaired condition.

Payments from Other Elements of Society.   Customers, lenders, investors, and others make payments to the reporting entity; in so doing they are sacrificing the utility that such purchasing power could command. This sacrifice is a cost to society vis-à-vis the reporting entity. Payments from customers might be netted against the value of the products and services provided, but the proposed unnetted or gross disclosure would be more informative—especially when market imperfections result in a significant difference between the value of products or services and the amount paid.

Other Costs. This catchall category includes any costs omitted above and provides flexibility to allow use of the model in many industries and under varying circumstances. One particularly important but unusual social cost, which belongs in this category but, unfortunately, will never be reported unless the report is prepared or at least audited by an external and independent entity, is the damage caused by political bribes, kickbacks, price-fixing, sabotage of competitors, and other forms of white-collar crime.

Products that fail to give adequate service or are unsafe can initially be accounted for in terms of reduced benefits, below the amount charged. Some products, dangerous drugs for example, may fail to provide any positive benefits and may in addition inflict costs; unsafe drugs may cause deaths, deformed births, or loss of organs. When the value of a product is actually negative, this cost may be included in this section.

Standard Footnotes

Several standard footnotes are proposed to report significant indirect effects and additional information that are relevant in judging an entity's effect on society but not additive in the model.

Significant Indirect Effects Associated with Inputs. Any social costs of goods and services used that are not reflected in exchange prices should be disclosed in this footnote. Examples are pollution caused by manufacturers in the production of materials used by the reporting entity, and air pollution caused by employees driving to work. As noted earlier, if complete social costs and benefits were internalized and integrated into the pricing structure of every entity, prices would reflect all social costs and this note would not be necessary.

Significant Indirect Effects Associated with Outputs. Pollution, injuries, solid waste, and other social costs resulting from the use of the reporting entity's products should be estimated and reported here. For example, in the report of an automobile manufacturer, the air pollution caused by automobiles should be noted here; since the pollution is not caused by the manufacturer directly, it is not included in the "cost" section of the report. Additional benefits should also be reported; this footnote is the proper place for disclosure by a producer of air-pollution-control equipment of the additional benefits to society derived from use of his products by customers. The direct benefit to the *customers* is of course included in the "benefits" section of the report and is not included in this footnote.

Bases for Measurements and Estimates.   Standardized measurement techniques are available or can be developed for many of the items in the body of the report, but several items will always require ad hoc techniques developed by the reporting entity. These should be described so that the reader can judge the reliability of the reported data.

Progress in Areas of Current Societal Concern.   This footnote should disclose the status, progress, and prospects of the reporting entity in areas of current concern to society. For example, disclosure should be made of efforts currently underway to reduce the pollution costs reflected in the body of the report, such as placement of an order for pollution-abatement equipment or initiation of pollution-reducing changes in the production process. Another example would be status and progress statistics on employment and promotion of minorities and women. Since matters reported here should reflect the social concerns of the period, they will change over time.

MEASUREMENT CONSIDERATIONS

While several measurement problems have been mentioned, much of the information needed for the proposed model is readily available in present financial information systems. Additional information can be systematically gathered with relatively minor system modifications. Some of the information needed, however, will require extensive system changes or expensive ad hoc studies. This disadvantage is partially offset by the likelihood that replications of studies are often much less expensive, and some studies can be done for an entire industry (possibly on a pooled cost basis or through an industry organization).

Measurement of social benefits and costs raises the question of comparing interpersonal utilities. This very complex question has received extensive attention in the economics literature, with many concluding that interpersonal utilities cannot be compared. In this chapter it is assumed that general or average measures of utility can be obtained.

The applicability of the proposed model hinges on the feasibility of several measurements, such as benefits derived from selected services, costs of various forms of pollution, and value of public services used. Chapter 5, which explores a number of approaches to and cases of social measurement, should serve as a useful guide—or at least a catalyst for ideas—for those undertaking such measurements.

SUMMARY

A social accounting model is proposed that would match direct benefits and costs generated by an entity, and show the resulting net surplus or deficit to society. The proposed model differs from the present financial reporting model and various proposed extensions primarily in its comprehensiveness; *all* significant direct benefits and costs to society would be reported, including those not presently internalized, such as consumers' surplus and air pollution. The model also differs in its viewpoint. Society's point of view would be taken; thus reported benefits and costs would reflect benefits and detriments *to society,* not to the firm.

The objective of the proposed model is to report fully the direct effects of the reporting entity on other elements of society and on society as a whole. Complete information should result in better evaluation of organizations by investors, policymakers, consumers, and citizens, and should thus contribute to more efficient resource allocation. Eventually the model might be used as a basis for a system of assessments and rewards to entities for their reported social surpluses or deficits, thereby internalizing present externalities.

A major advantage of the proposed model is that the socially responsible company would look better on the "bottom line" than its irresponsible competitor—a result exactly the opposite of that produced by the traditional financial income statement. The model should also prove useful to external entities—public interest groups, governmental agencies, the media—interested in evaluating the total impact of an organization on society.

In one sense, the proposed model represents a theoretical approach to potential assessment of the corporation's social impact, since measurement approaches are still being developed and social accounting measurement experience is limited. But experience in attempting to apply the proposed model to two entities—a complex not-for-profit entity and a profit-seeking manufacturing firm—suggests that reasonably satisfactory values can be obtained for almost all of the direct social benefits and costs. Thus the model should serve as a comprehensive format for the company contemplating public reporting of its effect on society, or simply attempting an internal assessment of its activities and role as a member of society.

*I have hardly ever known a mathematician
who was capable of reasoning.*

Plato, The Republic

5   Social Measurement:
Approaches and Cases

The greatest objection to social accounting is an apparent lack of valid and reliable measurement techniques. Accountants and businessmen often express an
acceptance of the general concept of corporate social accounting, but lack confi-
dence in their ability to assign suitable numbers to social effects. Corporate
executives responding to the Corson and Steiner survey cited inability to
develop acceptable measures of performance and inability to make creditable
cost/benefit analysis as the two most important obstacles to the development of
social audits.[1] This chapter describes several useful measurement approaches
and illustrates these with actual cases and results.

Social measurement often requires valuation of goods, services, and effects
that have not been exchanged in the market and consequently do not have
recorded exchange or market prices. Exchange prices are considered to be the
foundation of business accounting; businessmen and accountants have become
so accustomed to using exchange prices as a measure of value that it is difficult
for them to accept valuations not based on exchanges.

This is true even though a number of dollar values used by accountants do
not reflect exchange prices. Depreciation is a good example. Depreciation
allocates historical cost of an asset over its useful life in recognition of value
diminution from use and obsolescence. Were the accountant to abide strictly by
exchange prices, he would be required to carry assets at historical costs
unreduced by accumulated depreciation; depreciation is thus related to historical cost but is nevertheless an expense based on estimates (estimates of useful life, estimates of the rate of wear and tear, estimates of the obsolescence effect, estimates of salvage value), and not on market exchanges. The same is true

---

1 John J. Corson and George A. Steiner, *Measuring Business's Social Performance:
The Corporate Social Audit* (Committee for Economic Development, 1974), p. 36.

of bad debt expense, even though account balances derived from exchange transactions may enter into the estimate, along with historical patterns, economic conditions, and subjective assessments of account collectibility. Of course price-level adjustments, long advocated in the United States and now required in some countries, do not reflect exchange transactions, nor do current (or "fair") values that are used as the basis for valuation of marketable securities in the United States and as the primary basis for valuation of assets by some companies in The Netherlands.[2]

Despite the widespread reliance on exchange prices, they are not really very good measures of value, at least in the aggregate. The present market price of a good is generally taken to reflect the value of that good to the marginal customer—the one who would not buy at any higher price.[3] But with a downward sloping demand curve (the curve that applies to most goods) there are other customers who would be willing to pay more, and who benefit from a market price lower than their expected value for the good. This benefit, known as "consumers' surplus" and discussed more fully on the following pages, is not reflected in market or exchange price. Consequently, to measure the full value to purchasers of goods and services provided, we must add an estimate of consumer's surplus to revenue. As we shall see, it may be simpler to estimate total value directly, without regard to exchange prices, than to try to estimate the consumers' surplus increment.

Since exchange prices are often not available and are not very good indicators of social value anyway, we must resort to other measures of social benefits and costs. Occasionally we will find it necessary to develop original, ad hoc measurement approaches to capture unique social values. While first efforts are often not too impressive, the experience accumulated through repeated innovative attempts at social measurement can lead to measures that are as valid and reliable as many of the measures now used, reported, and attested to in financial accounting (such as the deferred income tax liability, joint cost allocations, amount of pension plan liability, depreciation, goodwill amortization, and allowance for uncollectible accounts). In applying previously tested techniques and in developing new ones, consultation with experts from other disciplines, including engineers, chemists, biologists, attorneys, physicists, sociologists, psychologists, physicians, and economists, may be warranted.

---

2 Current values, while certainly not the dominant basis of valuation, are nevertheless used to a surprising extent outside the United States, primarily to reflect significant changes in market value of fixed assets.

3 Or, the value of the last unit purchased to the customer who continues to buy until marginal utility, which would normally decrease with each additional unit, equals price.

GENERAL APPROACHES

Social measurement requires the estimation of benefits or utility provided by an entity, and the costs or sacrifices imposed on elements of society; we are thus concerned with the opportunity cost concept. It is not necessary to attempt to measure utility gained or sacrificed by every affected person, which would require the dubious technique of summing such utilities as if they were all comparable. It is normally sufficient to estimate *averages* for affected classes.

When measuring the effects of a single period, we must be alert for actions whose impact is spread over several years. Noise, if not so excessive as to inflict permanent damage, affects society only during the period of its existence, but materials consumed are lost to society for all the periods during which they might have provided utility. In the case of long-term effects, a discounting approach should be used to estimate the present value of the total impact. The relevant discount rate to be used is the highest return available to the affected elements of society.

Several general approaches are now briefly discussed. The reader may find that these techniques are not so unfamiliar, since they are similar to traditional market research efforts used to evaluate new products and to develop pricing strategies.

Surrogate Valuation

When a desired value cannot be directly determined, we may estimate instead the value of a surrogate—some item or phenomenon that is logically expected to involve approximately the same utility or sacrifice as the item in which we are interested.

Suppose that we are trying to estimate the value of building facilities loaned by a corporation to civic groups. We could obtain a surrogate valuation by determining the amount of rent such groups would have to pay if they rented commercial facilities having the same utility. Or we might be concerned with the value provided to purchasers of labor-saving construction equipment; as a surrogate we might estimate the cost of labor that customers would have to incur if this equipment were not available. Another example of surrogate valuation would be the use of commercial rates for equivalent recreational facilities to value free, company-provided recreational facilities.

With this method we must be careful to seek a surrogate *value* rather than a surrogate *price* (sometimes called a shadow price). We have already seen that prices generally understate value since they do not reflect consumers' surplus. Nevertheless, we may at times choose to accept a surrogate or shadow price when (a) no better estimate of value can be obtained, and (b) consumers' surplus is not expected to be large in relation to value. Even in such cases, however, we should qualify our valuation with the explanation that it is understated by some undetermined amount.

The danger of surrogate valuation is obvious: we are liable to measure the wrong thing, or select a surrogate that is not sufficiently related in value to the item under consideration. In spite of this danger, surrogate valuation is one of the most powerful tools available to the social accountant.

Survey Techniques

A number of survey techniques are available for social measurement. These involve obtaining information in some way from those affected—those elements of society who make the sacrifice or who receive the utility we want to value.

An obvious approach is to ask individuals directly what something is worth to them. This is a coarse and unsophisticated survey approach, but in certain circumstances it can provide information that is as usable as more sophisticated and thus more expensive techniques. For this direct inquiry method to be justified, several criteria must be met:

1. The user or affected individual must have a clear appreciation of the impact on him of the item under consideration.
2. He must be able to relate this impact to monetary units, either directly or through the use of surrogates.
3. He must be willing to give a truthful answer—or at least must have no discernible reason for lying.

Formulation of the questions is obviously critical with this technique. For social benefits they should take one of the two following forms: How much would you sacrifice to receive the item being valued? How much would you take to stop receiving the item? For social costs we ask: How much would you pay to avoid this detriment? How much money would you have to receive to induce you to endure it?

Some areas of social measurement may call for assessing the perceived value of a change in the *probability* of an event. Thus, rather than asking for the amount one would require to permit an event to occur (a probability of 1.0), we might ask about the cost of allowing the probability or risk to increase by, say, 10%. This refinement is especially appropriate in attempting to value injuries, disease, or human life. Many persons would value their life at infinity, but these same persons would accept a limited increase in the risk of death for some measurable amount. We find, for example, that automobile purchasers are often not willing to pay the extra charge for safety features that could prevent death or serious injury (such as dual braking systems or air bags), evidently because the extra charge exceeds their perceived expected value for the feature.[4]

In response to direct questioning respondents might reflect either of two biases. Some would attempt to inflate their status and wealth by indicating a willingness to pay that is higher than what they would actually be willing to pay; others would respond with an amount less than what they are really willing to pay for fear that a truthful answer might lead to a higher actual charge. The danger of these biases can be assessed in relation to the circumstances, the characteristics of the respondents, and the nature of the items being valued. When a significant possibility of bias is judged to exist, however, it may be preferable to use a *projective* technique. With this approach people are asked how much they think *others* would be willing to pay for the item in question. The projective technique should be effective in removing the upward bias, although a downward bias may still occur.[5]

Another extension of the direct question approach is to ask the respondent to locate or place the item of interest in an array of other items with established prices. This ranking may place the item of interest within a sufficiently narrow range to permit a reasonable estimation of value. With this approach we should capture the full value of the article, including consumers' surplus. To illustrate: suppose my utility function is such that I am willing to pay $8.00 for a dinner that is priced at only $7.00. If we use price as a measure of value, we understate value in this case by the amount of the $1.00 consumer's surplus. But if I am asked to locate this dinner in the following array:

$6.50
6.90
7.25
7.80
8.30
9.00

---

4 Suppose a device were available for $500 that would, with certainty, protect the driver in case of a specified type of accident, and a purchaser assessed his probability of having such an accident at .001 over the period of ownership of this automobile. If the purchaser bought this accessory, we could reason that he values his life at an amount equal to or greater than $500/.001, or $500,000. If he rejected the accessory, his valuation must be less.

5 However a study with which this author was associated revealed that financial analysts were willing to pay less for a hypothetical stock than their estimate of the market price; in other words, the respondents were willing to pay less than they thought others would pay. This result is probably an aberration, though, traceable to the financial analyst's self-image as one of greater sophistication than the average investor.

I shall place it between $7.80 and $8.30. Thus my response does not permit a precise valuation—value is located within a range of $0.49—but this result may be as precise as we can realistically achieve if respondents are not quite certain about their preferences.

An alternative form of this ranking approach, useful for obtaining an average value for a group of affected individuals, involves first dividing the group into several small subgroups. Each subgroup is then presented with a different price, along an ascending scale, for the item or effect of interest. (In the dinner example, subgroups might be presented with prices of $6.00, $6.50, $7.00, and so on.) Each individual is asked to respond to the price presented to his subgroup by indicating on a "reaction scale" the statement that best reflects his attitude toward this price. The results should indicate when a sizable resistance point has been reached, and might also be useful in supplementing other measurement approaches.[6]

Another variation of the ranking approach requires ranking of pairs of alternatives. Rather than having to array a number of items in order of preference, an individual merely has to be able to express a preference for one member of each of a number of pairs. The set of items used to create the pairs includes the item that we are trying to value plus a number of other goods with established market prices. Analysis of the responses should permit us to rank all the items in order of preference and thus estimate a value range for our item of interest. Unfortunately, this technique breaks down when the items selected do not possess the property of transitivity[7] for the respondent. This difficulty may be overcome by using one of the techniques discussed in the following paragraphs.

Greater precision is possible with the use of a system that calls for the assignment of weights to a set of items. This approach, variously called rating, weighting, cardinal ranking, or ratio scaling, involves first selecting a set of items, all familiar to the respondent and all but one (the item we are attempting to value) having established market prices. The respondent is then asked to

---

6 This technique, suggested by Dr. Henry Ostberg to Ruth P. Mock and Sumner Myers, is described briefly in their "Outdoor Recreation" in *Measuring Benefits of Government Investments,* Robert Dorfman, Ed. (Washington: The Brookings Institution, 1965), p. 86.

7 Transitivity may be viewed as a property of internal consistency, such that if A is preferred to B and B is preferred to C, then A is also preferred to C. Should C be preferred to A, we are faced with intransitivity, which may reflect an error of judgment or a misperception, or it may indeed reflect an intransitive utility function. This difficulty tends to disappear when we (*1*) use a large number of items and (*2*) emphasize monetary valuations over rankings.

arrange the items in order of preference and assign a weight to each, a weight that expresses his degree of preference or his perceived utility. The weight may simply be a number on a scale, or it may be a dollar amount. In the former case, weights are translated into dollars by first associating the established prices with the traded items and then valuing the remaining item according to its position on the scale. To illustrate, we might be concerned with the cost of noise near an airport. While we can deal with such a cost or negative value, it is easier to work with positive amounts, so we might instead consider the value of eliminating present noise. The list we present to a subject, with his resulting preference ordering and dollar assignments (on an annual basis), might appear as follows:

One new suit	$150
One steak dinner each month at the X restaurant	120
Trash collection service	100
Elimination of the airport noise	90
One movie every two weeks	75
Newspaper subscription for a year	50
Subscriptions to two professional journals	30

By presenting an array of items, most with established prices, our respondent is able to compare the items in question with other items with known utilities, and thus position the unvalued item among the others.

Using a similar approach, we could ask several subjects to each divide a given amount, such as $1000, among a list of items including the one in which we are interested. The requirements of assigning amounts to all items and making numerous interitem comparisons permits a subject to develop a clearer and more reliable impression of the utility of the item we want to value.

Finally, these ranking approaches may be used in a laboratory setting, with participants assuming behavior roles or perhaps engaging in competitive games. Implied values may then be obtained by observing actual decisions made.

Given the present undeveloped state of social measurement, many problems will require completely new valuation efforts. Nevertheless, we should be careful not to reinvent the wheel; work done by others may be directly relevant to our present needs. Examples of ongoing survey research that may be useful in social measurement are the public opinion polls such as those conducted by Daniel Yankelovich, Inc., and by Cambridge Reports, Inc. Other examples, dealing with past research, are presented later in this chapter.

Restoration or Avoidance Cost

Certain social costs may be valued by estimating the monetary outlay necessary to undo or prevent the damage. Some effects, such as pain and discomfort, cannot be undone. When these are involved, we must supplement the restoration cost estimate with estimates of such additional damage. But when the damage can be fully repaired or prevented, the restoration or prevention cost may represent the maximum amount we can reasonably assign to the effect. An example would be the damage to automobiles from the salting of streets in winter. The salt may cause extensive corrosion damage, but this damage may be prevented if cars are washed frequently. Suppose the damage to an unwashed car amounted to $300, but the cost of preventive washings would have been only $50; the $50 amount is the proper value to be assigned to this social cost. Terrain damage from strip-mining is another example; the cost of restoration to previous condition, including replacement of topsoil, is a reasonable maximum valuation for this damage (assuming that trees and valuable vegetation were not destroyed). Any higher valuation, based perhaps on the present value of lost crops, would be unsound since this higher cost can be completely avoided by incurring the lower restoration cost.[8]

Appraisals

Independent appraisals may be useful for valuing certain goods, buildings, and land. These will often reflect nothing more than an expert estimate of market value and are thus analogous to surrogate valuation performed by an outside expert. Appraisals may be appropriate for valuing donated goods, but most of the social benefits and costs we seek to measure in social accounting are not responsive to the appraisal approach. At any rate, when appraisals are used, we must be sure that we understand the basis for them and interpret the results accordingly. Property tax appraisals are often unrealistic, while other appraisals may be purposely biased to reflect some desired result (home appraisals, for instance, are sometimes "bent" to coincide with the desired selling price).

---

8 Restoration cost is a maximum value, not a minimum. If the aesthetic, recreational, and economic loss summed to less than restoration cost, we would use this sum. Note also that strip-mining may cause other damage, such as pollution of streams. For these effects we might use restoration cost *plus* a valuation for the interim effect on streams, reflected in dead fish and lost recreational opportunities.

Court Decisions

Awards for damages in court proceedings have an obvious appeal as indicators of social value. They are certain in amount and identified with specific social costs. While valuations based on such awards may be reasonable on occasion and may indeed reveal social attitudes concerning utility, we must keep in mind that the amount of the ultimate award is a product of the reasoning of third parties—judge or jury—and not of the injured person. Of course this person makes an appeal, through counsel, for an amount of damages, but given the accepted practice of pleading for some multiple of the amount actually sought, we cannot take this appeal seriously to indicate a value or sacrifice. We should use the amounts of awards in court decisions with considerable caution.

Analysis

Many times an economic and statistical analysis of available data produces a valid and reliable measure of value. Estimates of the increased earnings value of education have relied on present value analysis of comparative earning rates and life expectancies. Value (cost) of discrimination has similarly been estimated by calculating the present value of expected lost earnings for affected individuals.

Outlay Cost

Outlay cost to the acting entity is rarely a sound indicator of value to the affected entity, and is appropriately presented last in our list of measurement approaches. Cost of production incurred by a seller does not reflect the utility of the product to the buyer, even when cost of capital is added in. The temptation to use outlay cost seems greatest when valuing public programs, such as urban renewal, military defense, or highway construction; in these cases there is some merit in the argument that the collective decisions of society reflect society's expected utility. While outlay cost may be marginally appealing, we should nevertheless seek more direct and reliable measures of utility; even public expenditures are a function not only of expected utility but also of political considerations, pressure group activities, availability of funds, sophistication and knowledge (and even honesty) of legislators, and a variety of other factors.

APPLICATIONS AND CASES

Measurement approaches for the benefit and cost components of the comprehensive social reporting model introduced in Chapter 4 are now considered in some detail. Cases and research results are presented to demonstrate actual application of selected measurement approaches.

Several components of the model are easily measured; the exact technique to be used is often obvious from the circumstances. Other components—such as total value of goods and services provided, environmental impact, and cost of injuries and illnesses—are more difficult to estimate and are dealt with at greater length.

Total Value of Goods and Services Provided, Including Consumers' Surplus

The benefit rendered by an entity through sale of goods and services is measured by the total utility provided directly to customers; as noted earlier, this benefit is not adequately captured in exchange prices since they do not reflect consumers' surplus.

Consumers' surplus is value or utility received over the amount paid. We can intuitively accept the notion that goods such as lifesaving drugs, table salt, and many paperback books provide consumers' surplus. It may be less obvious that consumers' surplus occurs with every product that has a downward sloping demand curve, and this of course includes the vast majority of goods.

A typical demand curve is presented in Exhibit 5-1.[9] It is downward sloping, which indicates that larger quantities will be purchased only at lower prices. For instance, at price P_1 the quantity Q_1 is demanded or purchased; to induce buyers to purchase the quantity Q_2, the price must be lowered to P_2. With the lower price P_2, there are buyers who were willing to pay more (they would have bought quantity Q_1 at the higher price P_1) but who now receive the advantage of the lower market price; this advantage reflects consumers' surplus.

To illustrate, assume that my demand schedule for musical theater shows the following price/quantity relationships:

Price	Number of shows attended annually
$25	0
20	1
15	2
10	3
5	4

9 The demand curve in this case is drawn to intercept the Y-axis, which implies that there exists some price so high that none of the product will be bought. We have also used a straight line for simplification although we actually expect most demand "curves" to indeed be curved.

Now if the price is $20, I will attend one show and obtain $20 worth of benefits. But if the price is $5, I will attend four shows and obtain the following benefits:

	Benefits
First show	$20
Second show	15
Third show	10
Fourth show	5
Total benefits	$50

The cost of the four shows is 4 × $5, or $20, so my consumers' surplus is the difference between $50 in benefits and the $20 total cost, or $30.

Graphically, consumers' surplus is that area lying under the demand curve and above a line, parallel to the X-axis, extended from the Y-axis at the point of the present price to the demand curve. This is the shaded area PAB in Exhibit 5-2. (The supply curve has been added to this figure to establish the equilibrium price.)

We must keep in mind, however, that our objective is not merely to measure consumers' surplus; it is to estimate the *total* benefit received. Thus we need the sum of total sales revenue (price times quantity, or the area $OPBQ$ in

EXHIBIT 5-1

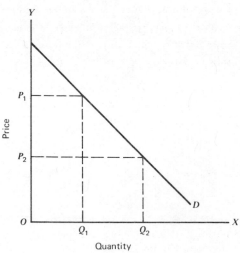

EXHIBIT 5-2

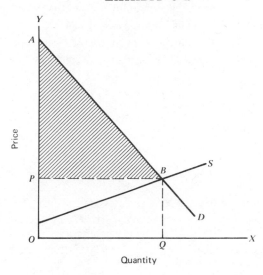

Exhibit 5-2) and consumers' surplus (the area *PAB*), or simply the total area *OABQ*.

Direct measurement of consumers' surplus requires construction of a demand curve or schedule. This demand curve must intercept the vertical (price) axis. These requirements have discouraged attempts at direct estimation of total consumers' surplus; however, the *change* in consumers' surplus has been estimated. A study of the benefits of a tunnel under the English Channel, published in 1963, concluded that a tunnel would produce an increase in consumers' surplus of £294 million.[10] A similar approach was taken in a New York City study to determine the effects of metering and charging, for actual water use, those customers who had been charged only a flat sum for water; it was concluded that the higher charges and reduced consumption resulting from metering would *reduce* consumers' surplus by about 7.5¢ per 100 cubic feet or some $20,000 in total.[11]

It may be easier to estimate directly the total benefit provided through the

---

10 £240 million for traffic diverted from other carriers plus £54 million for traffic newly generated by the lower costs. See E. J. Mishan, *Cost-Benefit Analysis* (London: George Allen & Unwin, Ltd., 1971), pp. 20–23.

11 George J. Stigler, *The Theory of Price* (New York: The Macmillan Company, 1966), pp. 80–81.

sale of goods and services; the approach we choose will depend to a degree on the nature of the product and the information that can be obtained. Abt Associates, Inc. (whose "social audit" was discussed in Chapters 2 and 3), reported their estimate of total benefits to clients from contract work in their 1971 "Social Income Statement" as follows:

	1971	1970
Social benefits to clients		
Added value of previous contracts to clients	$22,337,500	$12,870,000
Social costs to clients		
Contract revenues as opportunity costs	4,572,459	3,254,541
Net social income to clients	$17,765,041	$ 9,615,459

According to the footnote explanation, the "social benefits to clients" reflect Abt's estimate of the total value to clients from contract work in savings developed, resources mobilized, etc. The "social costs to clients" are simply Abt's contract revenues. Thus the "net social income to clients" is Abt's estimate of consumers' surplus provided.[12]

Abt tried to analyze the ultimate effects of its contract work and then to value these effects. This is obviously a difficult undertaking. An alternative for measuring benefits provided would require identification of alternative goods or services customers would be forced to use if those being valued were not available. For example, a well-planned computer installation may permit cost savings over manual data processing; these savings are consumers' surplus, and the total cost of manual processing can serve as a surrogate valuation for the computer installation. This approach was used by Nicole Zenz (then a graduate student at Wichita State University) in a study of the social impact of a Midwestern manufacturing firm. The firm produces equipment used in construction work; the practical alternative to the equipment is manual labor. Zenz thus calculated the labor hours displaced by equipment sold by the company, and priced these hours at the going rate, to arrive at an estimate of the total benefit provided by

---

12 Abt subsequently abandoned efforts to value consumers' surplus, although its 1973 and 1974 social audits reported benefits to clients equal to contract revenues plus unbilled employee overtime.

the company through sale of its equipment. This benefit was about seven times the sales price for the year studied.[13]

A deficiency of this approach can best be understood by reference to Exhibit 5-3. Present revenue is equal to price times quantity ($P_1 \times Q$), or the area OP_1BQ. The benefit calculated by Zenz can be described as the same quantity of work at the higher cost (*per unit of work or output*) of manual labor; this is $P_2 \times Q$, or the area OP_2CQ. But we have seen in our earlier discussion that the total benefit we want to measure is represented by the area $OABQ$. In her estimate, then, Zenz has included the triangle ECB (which does not enclose benefits) but excluded the benefit area P_2AE. These triangles will always have the same shape, but will be the same size only if the demand curve has a 45° slope (which of course is not the case in Exhibit 5-3). Zenz was able to satisfactorily resolve the problem in the case of this particular manufacturing concern by estimating that the difference in area between the two triangles was unlikely

EXHIBIT 5-3

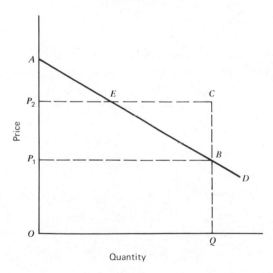

13 This approach credits the benefits of technological developments to the company that produces and sells the products, and in the year of sale. This seems appropriate when we consider that *society* does not benefit from newly developed or invented products until they are actually produced and sold. The labors of the scientist or the inventor are for naught if he does nothing with and tells no one of his discoveries. If he does make these available to a producing company, then of course *he* does provide a benefit to society at that point and should be so credited.

to be material (unlike the exaggerated representation in Exhibit 5-3). Whenever a material distortion is likely, we should study the historical sales/price relationships for the company and its industry to obtain some idea of the slope of the demand curve; once we have a reasonable estimate of this slope, the respective areas can be estimated and appropriate adjustments made.[14]

Numerous examples of efforts to estimate directly the value of benefits, as opposed to the surrogate approach just described, can be found in benefit/cost studies of public programs. For instance, in an application of the social accounting model described in Chapter 4, students in a graduate accounting research seminar sought to value the direct educational benefits provided by Wichita State University.[15] For a one-year period, this involved tabulation of enrollments by class, determination of differential expected annual earnings by year of college completed, actuarial calculations, and present value analysis. This is a particularly good illustration of the presence of consumers' surplus, for hardly anyone would argue that a college education is worth only what the student beneficiary pays for it.

Much work remains to be done before we shall have fully satisfactory techniques and data for measurement of total social benefits provided through the sale of goods and services, including the consumers' surplus portion. And of course much more synthesis of available research and statistics would be helpful. But the approaches discussed here, applied with careful consideration of the circumstances and a good bit of imagination, should produce useful benefit measures that will become more and more reliable as we add to our store of experience.

Employee Benefits

The primary employee benefit is of course employment itself. But even this may not be simple to value, for the benefit of employment includes all compensation plus training received, experience gained, and any positive psychic effects such as rewarding working conditions or special public respect associated

---

14 Greater precision can be obtained if a curvilinear demand function can be estimated. Unfortunately, this is usually unrealistic unless substantial historical data and perhaps market research results are available.

15 Other benefits and costs required by the model were also valued; these included research, employment, environmental effects, cultural contributions, and human resources used, among others.

with the work.[16] In addition there are the so-called fringe benefits, including Social Security, pension plan, and insurance contributions; unemployment taxes paid; workman's compensation insurance; educational assistance; and a host of other possible benefits. In valuing all these, we must remember to focus on the utility to the employee beneficiary, and not necessarily on the cost to the company or on some market price.

Direct compensation provides utility in the amount paid, or the outlay cost to the company.[17] Benefits provided through Social Security and pension plan contributions, unemployment taxes paid, and workmen's compensation insurance premiums or taxes should also be measured by the amount paid out by the company. Although this approach is not perfectly satisfactory, any other approach is probably unreasonable since the amounts paid go into funds supplemented and managed by various agencies and eventually used to provide benefits to a much broader range of workers than simply the company's employees. Even if the benefits were reserved for the company's employees (as with a private pension plan), the outside agency manages the fund and thus adds some incremental benefit of its own.

When a company makes payments for or on behalf of employees, the benefits provided should be roughly equal to the payment amounts, less some percentage to allow for those benefiting employees who would not have been willing to pay the full cost personally. A logical, subjective estimate of the appropriate reduction percentage should be adequate in many cases, although greater accuracy could be achieved with a questionnaire survey of a sample of

---

16 Under social costs we recognize the use of human resources, the other side of the benefit/cost coin. Psychologically negative aspects of the work as well as the basic sacrifice of time and effort are captured in this cost; more extreme conditions are covered in the separate costs of sickness and injury.

17 In the model presented in Chapter 4, payments for any purpose are treated as a benefit provided by the company to the recipient. If these payments in turn result in services or benefits provided to employees by third parties, such benefits are not separately counted as benefits provided by the reporting company, for to do so would result in double counting. However, if the reporting entity should purchase goods from a third party and pass these on to employees as gifts, the treatment in the model would be (1) payment to third party—a benefit to that party; (2) goods received from third party—a social cost to that party; (3) goods given to employees—a social benefit to employees. Thus a net benefit would be reported, which is what we would expect. In this section the constraints of the model are not so tightly observed, to permit a discussion of employee benefit measurement that is useful even if the social reporting model is not adopted.

employees. Thus a company may provide country club memberships for 30 executives at $1000 each year. Perhaps 20 of those executives would be willing to pay the full membership cost (ignoring possible consumers' surplus for simplicity, these 20 executives are each receiving a full $1000 benefit); the remaining 10 might be willing to pay a maximum of $500 of their own money. The total benefit provided is therefore 20 × $1000 plus 10 × $500, or $25,000. The $5000 difference ($30,000 − $25,000) is the excess of cost to the company over benefits provided (the area ECB in Exhibit 5-3). The appropriate reduction from outlay amount in this case would be $5000/$30,000, or about 17%. Gifts to employees should be treated in this fashion, and so should educational assistance payments such as tuition reimbursements.

Some benefits may be valued by the process of surrogate valuation, with a percentage deduction as described in the preceding paragraph. Training provided through formal programs or on-the-job training may be valued at the cost employees would have incurred for equivalent training at technical and vocational schools or at community colleges, again reduced by an estimated percentage for those who would not voluntarily incur such costs at going prices. This technique may be used to estimate the benefits of company-provided vacation retreats, use allowed to employees of company facilities and equipment, and company-sponsored sports activities and teams. The method is illustrated, although in another setting, by a study conducted in Canada by Touche Ross & Co. on the social value of recreational fishing. A questionnaire survey was used to determine how fishermen would compare the benefits from this activity with alternative recreational activities. A trade-off point was identified that indicated a family received on the average $135 in benefits per annum from recreational fishing.[18]

Certain company programs provide a clear savings to employees for necessities; these may properly be valued at the amount saved. Examples include a company cafeteria that provides greater convenience or lower prices than alternatives, company-subsidized housing, and perhaps medical and life insurance plans. The measurement steps are straightforward and require the identification of size and characteristics of the benefited group, the average price for the good or service without the company program, the average price charged by the company, and multiplication of the differential by the number of beneficiaries (beneficiaries may be broken into several classes for greater accuracy).

---

18 Gerald H. B. Ross, "Social Accounting: Measuring the Unmeasurables?" *Canadian Chartered Accountant,* July 1971, p. 5.

Analysis is an appropriate technique for valuing some benefits. Generally this will take the form of estimating savings or additional income over a period of future years, then discounting this stream to a present value. Experience provided by company employment, an obvious example, might be valued by estimating the increased earnings in each year of the employee's expected remaining work-life (based on actuarial tables, expected retirement ages, and turnover), discounted to present value by using the estimated highest rate of return available to employees on investments. Abt Associates used this approach in its 1974 social report; career advancement of employees was valued in terms of added earning power from salary increases for merit and/or promotion during 1974.[19] This technique might also be used in valuing medical and life insurance programs sponsored by the company; here again future benefits must be estimated with regard to mortality tables and probabilities of illness and injury, and then discounted to present value. Of course if we are measuring the firm's social impact for a one-year period, we must estimate the benefits from only that one year's insurance coverage.

Psychic benefits are a nebulous but important part of employment. Examples of psychic benefits include the following:

- Rewarding work conditions (resort work, possibly college teaching)
- Valuable "contacts" (White House Fellowships, working for a senator or in a political campaign, postdoctoral fellowships)
- Public respect (sports professionals, firemen, entertainers, journalists, political office prior to 1973)
- Feeling of power and authority (customs officials, police officers, airline pilots, politicians, doormen, military officers, sometimes accountants)
- Feeling of accomplishment and self-realization (artists, teachers, clergy, authors)

These examples overlap, of course, and some may be subsumed under experience in its broadest sense.

Measurement will always be difficult, in keeping with the intangible and rather personal nature of psychic benefits. The most promising approach appears to be the use of employee surveys conducted through questionnaires and interviews. A survey should seek to discover what type of employment (jobs,

---

19 The total of this benefit was estimated at $700,000 for 1974, up from $602,000 in 1973. See *Abt Associates Annual Report + Social Audit 1974.*

positions) an employee views as equivalent to his present work in terms of *total utility received.* If an employee presently earning $8000 per year as a public school teacher considers a sales position at $12,000 as providing equal total utility, we can judge that this teacher is receiving psychic benefits valued at $4000 (assuming nonpsychic fringe benefits are comparable in the two positions). Alternatively, we might choose several jobs that could reasonably be expected to provide zero psychic benefits; these might include ditchdigger, coal miner, janitor, payroll clerk.[20] We could then ask an employee: "Without regard to whether your answer is in line with present wage rates or whether anyone would pay you the amount you would require, how much would you have to make per year to leave your present job and become a ____ (coal miner, ditchdigger, etc.) ____?"

Occasionally circumstances will permit us to obtain a surrogate valuation for psychic benefits. This was done for faculty employment in the social benefit/ cost assessment of Wichita State University. It was reasoned that many professors accept salaries lower than they could earn elsewhere because of the rewarding nature of university employment. Census data were used to estimate the average annual earnings for individuals in various disciplines by level of academic preparation. These were aggregated to reflect the total potential earnings of the faculty at WSU in alternative employment. Actual total earnings were subtracted to produce a valuation for faculty psychic benefits equal to 18% of actual earnings (i.e., potential earnings were 118% of actual earnings).

Staff, Facilities, and Equipment Services Donated

Company employees contribute to society on behalf of the company when they perform services to community organizations, participate in professional activities, assist civic programs, and the like. The first measurement question is how to distinguish between benefits provided that should be credited to the company and those that should be credited to the individual. The distinction is not always easy to make, but as a general rule we can observe that activities undertaken either on company time or *in the role of employee* should be credited to the company. Here we would expect to find work done for a united charitable appeal, Chamber of Commerce activities, assistance to city government, most assistance to minority businessmen, and most participation in professional organizations. Strictly personal activities would include church

---

20 Of course each of these may be rewarding to certain people, but generally they are not desired positions.

work, PTA, Boy Scout work (unless perhaps the company sponsors a scout troup), and that portion of minority business assistance and professional organization participation that is undertaken solely on the employee's own volition and on his own time, and is not particularly encouraged or even noticed by the company.

The value of employee services donated, facilities provided to community groups, and equipment loaned out will only coincidentally equal the cost to the company. The real measure of value, as with all social benefits, is the utility received by the beneficiary. The most useful approach is to determine what such services would have cost the beneficiaries if they had hired them at market prices, and then to reduce this total by an allowance for any perceived unwillingness of the beneficiaries to buy the full quantity of services donated at the going market rate. Thus an executive who performs a clerical function for a charitable appeal would appear to provide benefits not exceeding the cost of temporary clerical help (regardless of that executive's salary). Facilities used by a community organization as a meeting place might be valued at the cost of equivalent facilities in, perhaps, the community library or a church basement.

In the social benefits and cost assessment of Wichita State University, it was necessary to value a host of services that were either provided free or at a nominal charge to the community, including meeting places, library privileges, drama programs, art exhibitions, certain athletic facilities, and various forms of entertainment programs. The basic approach used was to identify equivalent commercial programs and facilities, adjust the prices of these when they offered more or less evident utility, multiply these surrogate prices by the attendance or participation, and reduce the result by an estimated percentage to allow for those participants who would not have been willing to pay a full commercial price. Similarly, in a social assessment of a manufacturing firm, work performed at no charge (for either employee time or equipment) for church and civic groups was valued at the normal commercial charge less an adjustment of 15%.

Environmental Improvements

Occasionally it may be possible to improve on nature (heretical as this may sound) insofar as human benefits are concerned. Most of the environmental improvements we are concerned with, however, consist of undoing and repairing damage previously done by man, and improving on previous human construction efforts.

Sluggish and muddy streams may be dredged and rerouted to produce a more positive aesthetic effect, reduce flooding, and increase recreational fishing and boating opportunities, all to the benefit of humans. Corporations may landscape, provide playgrounds for employee children, develop and stock a company lake for recreational purposes, contour and plant previously eroded and treeless terrain, remove trash and junk from property, provide some form of flood control, turn previously used land into a wildlife refuge, and replace ugly structures with others that are more aesthetically appealing.

Public entities may do all of these things and often on a larger scale. With public or private entities, however, we must take care not to count as net "improvements" those changes that benefit only a few to the disadvantage of many. (For example, canalization of a river may provide cheaper bulk transportation to a limited number of corporations at a potentially greater aggregate cost to those who had used the river for fishing, boating, and hunting purposes or who were simply pleased to roam its shores.)

Improvements in previously negative conditions, which would have continued permanently if no action had been taken, should be included in this category. But reduction in continuous but nonpermanent detriments, such as air pollution, pollution to flowing streams, noise, and noxious odors, serve only to reduce the current period's social costs without creating a separate benefit. In other words, discontinuing a bad action doesn't count in this category; repairing the remaining and continuing effects of a previous bad action does.

Valuation of environmental improvements should be approached primarily through surveys of affected individuals and groups. Our procedure is to estimate the nature of effects on various groups, estimate the numbers affected, seek a measure of the average or mean degree affected, and translate this result into a money measure. The range of survey techniques discussed earlier in this chapter should be considered, including comparing the improvement with monetarily valued items, ordering and weighting a set including the environmental improvement being valued plus a variety of items with identifiable market prices, and allocating a given sum among members of such a set.

Goods and Materials Acquired

The direct social cost of goods and materials acquired is the sacrificed utility of the seller (or donor, in the case of goods acquired without payment). The *direct* social cost does not require any estimate of benefits to society at large from possible alternative uses of the goods and material; such benefits would be indirect as far as the acquiring entity is concerned.

Items with long useful lives, such as buildings, land, and equipment, should be treated in the same manner as raw materials and supplies in this calculation. The direct sacrifice to all of society outside of the acquiring entity is borne by the selling entity; the social cost to this seller is simply the present value of the item in alternative use or sale by him, and this is likewise true for short-lived goods. Thus we do not measure sacrifice to society in terms of annual depreciation as long-term assets are used; the sacrifice or cost to society occurs only once, on the date of acquisition. Annual sacrifices thereafter are only internal and are borne by the acquiring entity.

How do we measure a seller's sacrifice? Analysis of specific situations might be undertaken, with attention to the seller's alternatives of selling to a different buyer or retaining the goods for use. In rare cases this approach may be practical, but usually it is cumbersome and expensive. Our best approach appears to be the use of exchange price adjusted for producers' surplus.[21]

Producers' surplus is analogous to consumers' surplus discussed earlier in this chapter, except in this case exchange price overstates the value to the seller instead of understating value to the buyer. Suppose I am a wheat farmer willing to sell my wheat for $3.50 a bushel, but not willing to take less. The $3.50 establishes the wheat's value to me and my sacrifice (the social cost I incur) when the wheat is sold at whatever price. Other farmers, however, are holding their wheat in grain elevators until the price reaches $4.50. The demand for wheat is such that buyers quickly bid up the price to $4.50. Any wheat I sell at this higher price compensates me for my sacrifice at $3.50 per bushel (this is not the same as my cost of growing the wheat) and provides me with producer's surplus of $1.00 per bushel.

Producers' surplus is illustrated graphically in Exhibit 5-4. As before, straight lines have been drawn to represent supply and demand curves to simplify the presentation, and both curves have been assumed to intercept the vertical axis. The demand curve is presented to indicate the equilibrium price. In Exhibit 5-4 total proceeds to sellers is equal to $P \times Q$, or the area $OPBQ$. The sacrifice to each seller is the amount he would have accepted times the quantity sold; as illustrated in the wheat example, this will be less than the equilibrium market price for a number of sellers who thus obtain a windfall benefit from the interaction of aggregate market forces. The supply curve (labeled S) indicates the total quantity sellers would be willing to sell at each price, and thus defines the top limit of the sacrifice to each seller. The total sacrifice, or social cost to sellers, is the area $OABQ$ in the diagram. The shaded area APB is producers' surplus.

---

21 Otherwise known as economic rent.

EXHIBIT 5-4

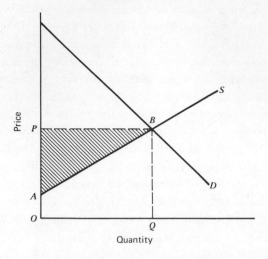

I have not been able to discover any useful studies of producers' surplus; available literature deals only with the theoretical formulation. Estimation approaches would appear to be similar to those suggested for consumers' surplus, however. Ideally, we would construct a supply schedule and curve reflecting quantities sellers would offer at different prices; historical price and quantity data might permit us to approximate such a curve. Otherwise, we may try to go behind the market data to obtain some estimate of the sacrifice incurred by the seller in terms of his cost function, including a reasonable return on investment. As a last resort we may make a rough subjective estimate. This at least forces our attention to the issue, and with some experience will probably provide results that are not seriously distorted.

Services Used

This category includes all human services used by the reporting entity—services of laborers, services of executives, services of outside professionals.

Traditional benefit/cost analysis usually seeks to value human services in terms of their next best available use, on the grounds that the product of the next best alternative is sacrificed by society because of the existing or proposed employment. The focus in traditional analysis is thus on indirect effects—sacrifice of alternative production by society at large—rather than the direct effect on the employee. For our purposes the focus should be on the direct sacrifice by the individuals providing services to the company.

Fortunately, the incorrect *focus* of traditional analysis may on occasion produce correct results. We are interested in a dollar valuation of the sacrifice to the employee for his time and effort. This sacrifice is measured by the value to him of the best alternative use of his time and effort. Alternative uses include work, play, study, relaxation, and so forth. Barring some sort of coercion, we can assume that the employee's present employment reflects his judgment as to the *best* alternative, the one that provides him with the greatest utility. We would thus expect the second best alternative to carry a lower value, and the total benefits obtained from his present employment to therefore exceed his sacrifice or cost.

In measuring the social cost of services used, we might undertake a supply analysis with the objective of developing a supply schedule and curve. The area under this curve would represent the social cost imposed on those whose services are used. We could as a matter of interest also calculate the amount of producers' surplus created by present employment patterns—the area *APB* in Exhibit 5-4.[22] This separate calculation is unnecessary, however, since the amount of producers' surplus is reflected in the *difference* between total benefits provided to employees and others whose services are used, and total sacrifice or cost to them. This difference increases the net social surplus in the social reporting model of Chapter 4.

As an alternative approach to estimation of social costs from services used, we might use the value of the total benefit package to employees and then reduce this, perhaps by an estimated percentage, to account for less desirable alternative employment opportunities available on the average. If we use this approach, we must take care to begin with a fair estimate of the *total* benefits provided including all fringe benefits, experience provided, and psychic income; direct monetary compensation alone significantly understates total benefits.

In the social assessment of Wichita State University, census data were used to estimate potential alternative earnings for faculty members having different levels of education and different disciplines and professions.[23] A similar approach, relying on census data and local economic and employment statistics, should be feasible for business firms.

Although not of immediate use, studies that develop a valuation for units of

---

22 Producers' surplus results both from the interaction of demand and supply forces, and from factors supporting compensation at an amount higher than that required by the supply schedule, such as minimum wage laws, union contracts, company policy to pay good wages, or even nepotism.

23 Greater accuracy would have resulted if experience factors could also have been taken into account, but data necessary for this refinement were not available.

time may eventually provide us with data useful for valuing employees' sacrifice. One such study estimated the value of time for intercity passengers at $3.00 per hour, based on a survey and synthesis of 14 previous studies.[24] This is the upper end of a range of values reported for average automobile passengers. The value of time for the urban commuter was estimated at the lower end of the range, at $1.50 per hour.[25] Another study estimated the value of time to travelers in the Northeast Corridor of the United States at $13.50 per hour.[26] The large differences between the two studies are apparently because the former was concerned with commuters' time while the latter was concerned with the time of travelers traveling on business, where the sacrifice might be greater.

Discrimination

Discrimination in employment costs the individual and the nation. Our model in Chapter 4 calls for estimating the direct effects on individuals against whom discrimination is practiced, but we ought to take note of the indirect effects even if these are not reported in the model. Estimates of the indirect costs to the nation vary but are always huge. An early study by E. Roper, reported by Becker in 1957, estimates the loss to the nation by discrimination against Negroes at $4 billion of real wealth per year.[27] A more recent study by the Equal Employment Opportunity Commission estimated that if nonwhites were upgraded to the same employment levels as whites, annual productivity would be increased by $30 billion.[28] We are constantly hearing calls to increase productivity, especially when business faces inflation and higher wage costs. What better way to increase productivity than by eliminating discrimination?

For social accounting purposes it is helpful to divide employment discrimination into two parts: discrimination in hiring, or external discrimination; and

---

24 J. R. Nelson, "Values of Travel Time," in *Problems in Public Expenditure Analysis,* Samuel B. Chase, Ed., (Washington: Brookings Institution, 1968); cited in *Benefit Cost Analysis 1971* (Aldine, 1972), p. 440.
25 *Ibid.*
26 U. S. Department of Transportation, *Passenger Demand and Modal Split Models,* Northeast Corridor Transportation Project Report No. NECTP-230, Washington, December 1969; cited in *Benefit Cost Analysis 1971, ibid.,* p. 440.
27 G. Becker, *Economics of Discrimination* (Chicago: University of Chicago Press, 1957), pp. 22–23.
28 Equal Employment Opportunity Commission, *Second Annual Report,* H.R. Doc. No. 326, 90th Cong., 2d Sess. (1968), p. 1.

discrimination against employees in placement, advancement, training, and the like, or internal discrimination.

External discrimination imposes direct costs upon those women and minorities who would have been hired if discrimination had not occurred. Its cost is measured by their loss in income and their exclusion from experience opportunities and other positive aspects of employment (including psychic effects.)

The observation that discrimination is difficult to measure in monetary terms is certainly not profound. The cost to the individual is due to an amalgamation of past discrimination pervasively reaching to schools, employment, government, and indeed every aspect of community life; the present pattern of discrimination throughout society, including discrimination by other employers; and a particular company's prior history with respect to employment for minorities and women. Statistical studies could be devised to isolate these various effects, but to my knowledge none have yet been attempted.

A direct, if cumbersome, approach to estimating the social cost of external discrimination might involve the following steps:

1. A careful analysis of the company's present employees and positions, and an estimate of probable levels of employment of minorities and women at each level if discrimination had never existed in the company.
2. Calculation of the gap between potential and actual employment at each level.
3. Analysis of community employment patterns and opportunities, as a basis for estimates of alternative employment opportunities for those discriminated against.
4. Calculation of the deficiency in compensation and employment benefits for available alternative employment.
5. Calculation of the total cost of company external discrimination by a multiplication of the results of step 4 by those of step 2. If an annual report is produced using a flow (benefits/cost) rather than a stock (balance sheet) approach, then the result of this step should be allocated between the present and prior years.

Step 3 in this process would be the most difficult. Statistics permitting the conversion of employment deficiency levels by race and numbers into dollars would certainly be useful. One study provides us with amounts that appear sufficiently generalizable to permit their use in many companies. In a study released in 1957, the Economics Reasearch Center at the University of Chicago estimated the loss to blacks due to discrimination at roughly 16%; that is, blacks would earn 16% more if no discrimination occurred.[29] Since it is difficult to determine the present incomes of those blacks whom a company may have discriminated against, we would prefer to know how much less blacks make than present employees—what percentage of the present payroll reflects discrimination in favor of present employees. Becker gives this as 13%.[30]

We might use this result as follows. Suppose we determine that in new hiring this year, our company has discriminated against blacks to the extent of 15 entry-level positions, each earning an average of $6000 per year. The blacks who didn't obtain these jobs are assumed to be earning 13%, or $780, less. The social cost of external discrimination for this year is therefore 15 × $780, or $11,700.

The cost of internal discrimination is a little easier to get a handle on, though still difficult to estimate. In this case we can focus our attention on only those minorities and women already employed by the company. If the number of such employees is small, our analysis can proceed individual by individual; if it is large, we may prefer to use statistical analysis.

Precisely what should we include in the social cost of internal discrimination? It is the cost to employees due to the negative action of discrimination during the period under consideration. For a one-year period, the social cost is the present value of lifetime sacrificed income and experience due to a delay in advancement of one year. This is not to say that we are confident advancement will occur in the following year (although it is certainly more likely once discrimination has been identified); but discrimination in the following year is calculated separately and charged to that year—in fact this procedure should be followed for every period.

The procedure can be illustrated by an overly simplified example. Assume that, through discrimination, one person (presently earning $10,000 per year) was passed over for advancement during the year just ended. The compensation increment with each promotion is assumed to be $2000; otherwise she can expect a raise of $1000 each year. For simplification we place no value on the higher level of experience associated with advancement. Using actuarial tables and company employment experience, we estimate this employee's remaining

---

29 Becker, *op. cit.*, pp. 22–23. Becker notes that other estimates have been much higher, but ascribes the difference to whites' greater capital per capita, so that even without discrimination whites would receive higher incomes. We can of course question whether the whites' higher capital levels don't also reflect past discrimination patterns. At any rate, Becker's figures can be taken as conservative, a *minimum* loss to blacks.
30 *Ibid.*

term with the company at nine years. We also estimate that advancements normally occur every three years. The employee may invest her money in secured bonds at 8%. Exhibit 5-5 shows the calculations that produce our estimate of employee's sacrifice at being discriminatorily passed over for advancement this year, $2244. We can see from this table that the cost of one year's internal discrimination is the present value of one year's delay in each future promotion (assuming that no further discrimination occurs).

Abt Associates, Inc., estimated the social cost of external discrimination at $1000 in its 1974 social report (reproduced in Chapter 2). This amount was described as the total difference between what each minority or female individual earned and what a nonminority or male individual with the same qualifications doing the same job earned.

The cost of internal discrimination, or discrimination in pay and advancement, was estimated in studies at Rutgers University and at Southern Methodist University. In the Rutgers study, multivariate regression analysis was performed utilizing such factors as sex, race, years of service, years since receipt of highest degree, number of professional articles and books published, and division and department of the university. It was found that discrimination was costing women about $500 per year on the average.[31] The SMU study used multiple correlation analysis and produced comparisons of male and female salaries for various qualifications and departments. About three fourths of the women faculty members were found to have salaries markedly below those of men having corresponding academic credentials and productivity, with the deficiency ranging as high as 50%.[32]

These studies provide good examples of the use of statistical analysis when the number of employees is too great to permit analysis individual by individual, and especially for organizations with a large number of professional-type employees whose qualifications can be readily cataloged.

Other indications of the cost or value of discrimination can be found in damage judgments against some of the largest corporations of America; as noted earlier, however, these do not necessarily represent the accurate cost to those discriminated against.

Discrimination costs are difficult to estimate, but fortunately much of the

---

31 Georgina M. Smith, "Faculty Women at the Bargaining Table," *AAUP Bulletin,* Winter 1973, pp. 402–406.
32 Barbara B. Reagan and Betty J. Maynard, "Sex Discrimination in Universities: An Approach Through Internal Labor Market Analysis," *AAUP Bulletin,* March 1974, pp. 13–21.

EXHIBIT 5-5

Year	Annual Earnings Without Discrimination	Annual Earnings With Discrimination	Difference	Present Value Factor*	Present Value of Difference
1	$12,000	$11,000	$1000	0.926	$ 926
2	13,000	13,000	—		
3	14,000	14,000	—		
4	16,000	15,000	1000	0.735	735
5	17,000	17,000	—		
6	18,000	18,000	—		
7	20,000	19,000	1000	0.583	583
8	21,000	21,000	—		
9	22,000	22,000	—		
					$2244

* Based on discount rate of 8%. Earnings are assumed to have been received in total at end of each year; adjustment may easily be made to reflect earnings received evenly throughout the year.

basic data will already have been compiled in most companies for Form EEO-1 required by the Equal Employment Opportunity Commission.

Injuries, Illness, and Death

We come now to a form of social costs that many will argue cannot and should not be valued in terms of money; good health, and life itself, are invaluable. Any effort to assign dollar values to them is crass and degrading.

As appealing as these arguments may be, we cannot deny that decisions are made daily that affect safety, health, and the likelihood of death—public decisions such as safety requirements for airplanes, automobiles, and consumer products; corporate decisions such as how much money will be spent for safer and more healthful working conditions; and personal decisions like whether to buckle seat belts. These decisions can be made with the best information available and can reflect rational trade-offs, or they can be made subjectively, irrationally, on hunch or whim or personal bias.

Benefit/cost studies have typically relied on estimates of the present value of expected future earnings lost as a result of injuries, illness, and death, probably because these data have the appearance of objectivity. In other words, the cost to the affected person and his family is measured by income lost. Others have used the present value of production lost to society. A refinement is to use the present value of expected future earnings less expected consumption; the rationale behind this approach appears to be that a worker produces goods for society equal in value to his earnings, but only the excess of such production over the worker's consumption is left for society's benefit. In other cases the amount of life insurance purchased by an individual has been used as an indicator of the value he places on his life.

These approaches are all deficient because they either measure the wrong things or they fail to measure enough of the right things.

The direct cost to society of work-related injuries and illness is the sum of (*a*) the present value of expected lost earnings, (*b*) the present value of lost experience, (*c*) the present value of the cost of delayed promotions, (*d*) out-of-pocket costs to the injured, primarily uninsured medical expenses, (*e*) insurance proceeds (a cost to the insurance company), and (*f*) the net value of pain and suffering. This last factor is usually ignored, but its importance is readily apparent when we consider how much we would have to be paid to undergo a given injury or illness—a broken leg, for example—if we could be assured that we would miss no work, lose no earnings, and incur no out-of-pocket costs because all medical bills would be covered by insurance. Would we be willing to have a leg broken with no compensation—or would we require $50, $100, $500, or more?

This example suggests the most effective method of getting at the value (cost) of pain and suffering. A representative sample of employees may be surveyed to determine the amount each would pay to avoid, or the amount each would require to induce him to undergo, a given illness or injury. The average response should capture any expected lost earnings and experience, expected out-of-pocket costs, and an amount for pain and discomfort. The responses should take into account such compensatory factors as medical insurance, workman's compensation, and Social Security, although we may want to discuss these thoroughly with each subject before eliciting his response, to be sure that he has adequately considered them. It is also desirable to obtain enough observations to permit calculation of average values for different age groups, ethnic groups, economic classes, and the like.

Another, less promising, approach is to determine amounts actually paid by individuals to guard against or reduce the risk of injury or illness. Such payments include the cost of medical checkups, vaccinations, safety shoes, protective goggles, preventive drugs, helmets, and the like. For example, we might determine that three fourths of our employees are willing to pay $3 each for flu shots; the shots are reputed to be 50% effective; and the likelihood of contracting flu without the shots is estimated by the employees, on the average, at 1 in

10, or 10%. We can now calculate

$$P = C \times L \times E$$

where P = prevention payment,

  C = cost of flu to employee (if actually contracted),

  L = likelihood of contraction without preventive shots,

  E = effectiveness probability of shots.

In this example, we have

$$\$3 = C \times .10 \times .50$$

Solving for C,

$$C = \frac{\$3}{.10 \times .50} = \$60 = \text{the perceived minimum cost to}$$
three fourths of the employees
of contracting flu.

Some of the data needed for calculating the social cost of work-related injuries and illness are already required by the Occupational Safety and Health Act of 1970 for OSHA Form 103; however, further detail as to incidence of injury and illness by type must be collected prior to attempting to assess costs.

Assessing the value for life (a cost of death) is even more controversial than dealing with injuries and illness. Some assert that life is priceless and refuse to argue further. I personally tend to view efforts to value life as dangerous, contributing toward an elitism that holds lives in certain social classes to be more valuable than others and even encouraging a "superman" mentality. Nor am I at all sure who bears the sacrifice of death; is it society at large, the surviving friends and relatives, or the decedent—and as to the latter, what does death matter after the fact? But this reluctance to enter the controversy is tempered by concern that current approaches to this valuation are conceptually wrong and may lead to grave policy errors.

As noted earlier, the cost of death is not adequately reflected in (*a*) present value of expected future earnings, (*b*) present value of production lost to society, (*c*) present value of expected future earnings less expected consumption, or (*d*) amount of life insurance purchased by an individual. The first three approaches ignore the individual's own feelings about death, his pain and suffering, and survivors' bereavement. The premium cost of life insurance indicates neither the amount one would pay to avoid death (since life insurance of course does not prevent it) nor the value one places on his life (it indicates more about his feelings for beneficiaries).

The direct cost of death, to those immediately affected, includes the following:

1. Out-of-pocket medical costs (we may consider part of these as not incremental but only premature, insofar as even death from old age involves medical expenses).

2. Premature burial cost, that is, the present cost of burial minus the present value of burial cost at actuarially expected date of death.

3. Present value of income of the decedent lost to his or her family (there is room for argument about including this, since the income is a benefit provided by the decedent to his or her family, but work-related death deprives the family of this income and this deprivation is thus traceable to the company).

4. Payments by insurance companies (costs to the companies but not to the next-of-kin or deceased).

5. Bereavement of survivors and friends.

6. The value an individual places on his own life.

Inclusion or exclusion of this last cost appears to depend on whether we are considering death *ex ante* or *ex post*—before or after the fact.[33] Generally, I believe we should include it. It will be noted that cost to society beyond those directly affected—in terms of lost production—is not listed here because this is an *indirect* cost, and our model excludes indirect costs.

Costs 1, 2, 3, and 4 are susceptible to evaluation through analysis. General estimates for cost 5 may be obtained through surveys, although this or any other technique is of doubtful validity for this most difficult and sensitive element. Bereavement is usually intense but short-lived except for those very close to the decedent.

We can approach estimation of the value an individual places on his own life in the same general way we approach valuation of injuries and illness. We first observe that humans do not seek to avoid risk of death at any cost; our daily lives are replete with risks that we undergo willingly enough in return for the benefits of our activities (examples of such risks include crossing a street, flying, swimming, horseback riding, smoking, and any heart-taxing exertion). Some activities and occupations appear to reflect conscious, if subjective balancing, of

---

33 It may also depend on metaphysical arguments that even *social* accounting cannot deal with.

risks against benefits:[34] Evel Knievel's daredevil motorcycle jumps, high-wire circus performances, test pilots, combat pay, auto racing.

We can next use either of two techniques to establish the value of an increment of risk. We can survey individuals to try to determine the amount they would require to accept a specified increase in risk. Or we can observe the incidence of purchases that reduce the risk of death, such as air bags in new automobiles, dual braking systems, tornado shelters, medical treatment (including physical examinations), and life preservers for boats. With either approach we seek an average dollar amount associated with a specified risk increment.

Finally, we extrapolate these data into totals. If we assume a linear relationship between risk and value, as in Exhibit 5-6, the calculation is simply:

$$V = \frac{\$}{R}$$

where $ is the amount associated with a given risk increment R. Thus if I purchase a new automobile equipped with air bags at an extra cost of $300, and I expect the air bags to reduce my risk of death by .001 (the odds of my having an accident in this car that an air bag will enable me to survive are 1 in 1000), then implicitly I value my life at $300/.001, or $300,000.

Unfortunately, the relationship between risk and value is unlikely to be linear. As shown in Exhibit 5-7, it probably increases slowly for changes from one low level of risk to another, but then increases at an increasing rate as risk of death nears 1.0, perhaps becoming vertical and suggesting a willingness to incur *any* cost to avoid the certainty of death. Studies could be devised to determine the general shape of this curve, but to my knowledge none have as yet been undertaken.

Cases of injury or illness valuation invariably understate the cost by omitting the major factor of pain (discomfort, inconvenience, frustration, suffering). For example, Ridker considered only cost of treatment (at per capita value of drug shipments) and absenteeism (as the product of days lost times the average annual earnings of those suffering).[35] Reede's study of workman's compensation

---

34 Precisely formulated such decisions indicate that

$$(1 - P_d)(B) \geq (P_d)(V_d)$$

where P_d = probability of death from the activity,
  B = expected incremental benefit from the activity if death doesn't occur,
  V_d = cost of death, or the value one places on his life.

35 Ronald G. Ridker, *Economic Costs of Air Pollution,* (New York: Praeger, 1967), pp. 30–56.

EXHIBIT 5-6

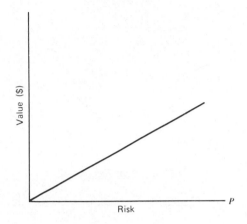

in Massachusetts dealt only with lost wages.[36] Estimates by the National Safety Council in 1942 on accident prevention concentrated on production lost—these indicated an average cost to the economy in terms of production lost of $1000 per accident, or approximately $82 per man-day lost, in 1942 dollars.[37] Adjusted for price-level increases, these amounts would be approximately $2662 per accident and $218 per man-day lost, in 1973 dollars.

Value of life estimates also tend to concentrate on economic effects exclusively, with no regard to personal factors, pain, or bereavement. One rather thorough calculation estimated the "value" of an air-carrier fatality in 1960 at $373,000, and the value of a general-aviation fatality in that year at $422,000.[38] The $373,000 amount is the sum of estimates of lost earnings (based on an average salary of $13,000, a yearly increase in salary of 2½%, assets of $25,000, an average age of death of 40, and a discount rate of 6%); economic loss to the decedent's family; and loss to the community, his employer, the government, and the airline. In a somewhat different approach, statisticians at the National Highway Traffic Safety Administration calculated the amount "society could reasonably be expected to pay to protect a life" at $200,000.[39]

---

36 A. H. Reede, *Adequacy of Workman's Compensation* (Cambridge: Harvard University Press, 1947), p. 212.
37 William K. Kapp, *The Social Costs of Private Enterprise* (New York: Schocken Books, 1950), p. 52.
38 Gary Fromm, "Civil Aviation Expenditures," in Dorfman, *op. cit.,* pp. 172–216.
39 *Business Week,* October 14, 1972, p. 41.

EXHIBIT 5-7

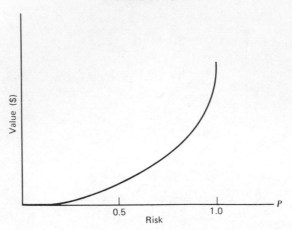

We have already mentioned the unsuitability of court judgments for valuing injuries, illness, and life. It may nevertheless be interesting to consider such awards to compare the opinions of judges and juries with results of research studies. A California jury recently awarded $1,850,000 for four deaths resulting from airplane crashes, exclusive of any punitive damages;[40] this works out to $462,500 per death, not out of line with the estimates obtained through other approaches. And a jury recently awarded $392,500 to a roofer who lost his left arm in an industrial accident;[41] the magnitude of this award suggests that partial disablement is viewed as nearly as costly to the individual as death itself.

The work done to date on quantifying the cost of injuries, illness, and death does not provide us with the reliable averages we need to measure the impact of a corporation on the health and safety of its workers and the community. We need a number of studies dealing with the more common results of corporate activity, and reflecting differences by age, economic, ethnic, and worker group. This section has suggested the techniques—survey research and observation of safety-oriented behavior—that should be useful in conducting these studies.

Environmental Damage

Environmental damage occurs in a variety of forms. Air pollution may cause physical damage to structures, loss in property values, pain, and discomfort.

---

40 "Beech Suit is Settled," *Wichita Eagle,* August 8, 1974.
41 "Loss of Arm Is Worth $392,000," *Wichita Eagle,* March 8, 1974.

Water pollution results in greater costs of treating water for human consumption, kills fish and plant life, reduces contiguous property values, and reduces the aesthetic appeal of rivers and streams. Erosion reduces the utility of land and, consequently, its resale value. Noise and odor pollution are unpleasant and sometimes unhealthy, and also reduce property values. "Aesthetic" pollution includes unsightly structures as well as air and water pollution.

The most promising approaches to measurement of environmental damage are surveys, analysis, and estimation of prevention or restoration cost.

Surveys may be used to determine the amounts people would pay to avoid pollution or the amounts they would have to be paid to endure pollution. The survey approach may also be used to obtain actual experience data from persons who have experienced environmental damage costs. Following malfunction of boilers at the Syracuse University power plant, which subjected the neighborhood to unusually high amounts of soot, 122 residents were interviewed to determine the costs of cleaning up and also their willingness to pay to avoid the need for such cleaning in the future. Willingness-to-pay costs were equal to or greater than the actual measured cleanup costs (which averaged $7.10 per household) in all cases.[42] Williams and Bunyard used the survey approach in a 1963 survey to determine the amount residents in the St. Louis area were willing to pay for clean air; they determined that 66% were willing to pay as much as $5 per year while 85% were willing to pay at least $1 per year.[43] The same approach was used by Lawyer in a 1965 study in Morgantown, West Virginia, where air pollution is more of a problem than in St. Louis. Lawyer found that, on the average, residents were willing to pay $16.46 per year to reduce air pollution; 13.5% of the respondents were willing to pay as much as $40 annually.[44]

Analysis is an encompassing technique that seeks to pull together information from a variety of sources. For example, the cost of air pollution to homeowners might be estimated by an analysis of lost market values. One extensive study of this sort correlated local concentrations of sulfur dioxide, ash, and soot in the air with the decline in property values in 85 cities.[45] It concluded that a 1% increase in airborne dirt led to a decline in property value of 0.8%. Similarly, in separate analyses, Ridker, and Lave and Seskin developed estimates of the annual health costs of air pollution; Ridker estimated total annual

---

42 Ridker, *op. cit.,* pp. 90–114.
43 Larry Barrett and Thomas E. Waddell, *Cost of Air Pollution Damage: A Status Report* (Research Triangle Park, North Carolina: U.S. Environmental Protection Agency, 1973), p. 46.
44 *Ibid.,* pp. 46–47.
45 "The Price of Pollution," *The Journal of Accountancy,* July 1973, p. 64.

health costs in 1958 at approximately $2 billion, while Lave and Seskin's estimate for 1963 was only slightly higher, at $2.08 billion.[46]

Partial costs of water pollution have been estimated through analysis of the number of fish killed and their market value.[47] The annual cost of noise in the United States, based on an analysis of compensation payments, accidents, inefficiency and absenteeism, has been estimated at $4 billion.[48] Numerous other examples could be cited, but it should be clear that analysis is a powerful tool for estimating social costs and benefits from existing data.

In social accounting we are generally concerned with measuring the benefits and costs actually experienced. In some cases, however, it may be appropriate to use as a surrogate for actual costs the costs that would have been required to *prevent* the damage; this would seem especially appropriate when the damaged entities could have prevented such damage by taking preventive action. For example, if an employee could have prevented an industrial injury by purchasing safety equipment, then the cost of such equipment would be a reasonable maximum charge to the company for the social cost of the accident. Perhaps the company should have provided the equipment or should have developed safer processes; the employee nevertheless had the power to limit his loss to the cost of equipment. That he chose not to was his decision, and the additional cost attributable to this decision should not be charged to the company.

Much the same reasoning applies to the use of restoration cost—the cost of repairing or undoing damage done. If this approach is used, however, we must be careful to include the cost from the time the damage is done until it could possibly be repaired.

Examples of avoidance cost estimates include the numerous calculations of cost of air-pollution control and abatement equipment, water treatment facilities, and noise mufflers. The U.S. Departments of the Interior and of Health, Education & Welfare estimated the cost to control water, air, and solid waste forms of pollution in the United States at $71 billion over a five-year period (1970 to 1975).[49] Similarly, estimates prepared for the Aviation Advisory Council show that it would cost $1.3 to $1.6 billion per airport to move residential land uses away from airports to avoid the noise and pollution.[50]

The cost of "repairing" the damage of air pollution might include medical

46 Barrett and Waddell, *op. cit.,* pp. 8–10.

47 "High Cost of Dying," *Sports Illustrated,* October 8, 1973, p. 14.

48 "Clamor Against Noise Rises Around Globe," *The New York Times,* September 3, 1972.

49 "Pollution Price Tag: 71 Billion Dollars," *U.S. News & World Report,* August 17, 1970, pp. 38–42.

50 Council on Environmental Quality, *Environmental Quality—1973,* p. 76.

expenses, painting, cleaning, refinishing surfaces, and so on. The concept of undoing water-pollution damage is a bit easier to grasp and the cost more amenable to estimation. The cost of primary treatment per 1000 gallons of water, with removal of one third of the biochemical oxygen demand (BOD), has been estimated at about 3 to 4¢; the cost of secondary treatment, with removal of 90% of BOD, 33% nitrogen, and 33% phosphates goes up to 15 to 20¢ per 1000 gallons.[51] In the Ruhr Valley water resources cooperative associations (Genossenschaften), water polluters are assessed an effluent charge equal to estimated downstream damages (resulting from increases in water supply treatment and the value of physical damages).[52] Kapp cites 1934 estimates of $12 to $20 million annually for repair and replacement of locomotive boilers due to acid pollution in the water.[53]

Demonstrating that visual or aesthetic pollution has an estimable cost, residents of a northern Illinois community went to court to force the telephone company to remove overhead lines and place them underground; the substantial cost would of course eventually find its way back to the customers/residents through increased charges, but they were evidently willing to bear these charges to avoid the eyesore. And a number of states are requiring strip miners to restore mined areas through replacement of topsoil, grading, and planting of tree seedlings; these requirements can be taken to reflect a collective decision that the cost of strip-mining damage is sufficient to warrant the cost of required reclamation.

Surrogate valuation and shadow pricing may have some application in determining the social cost of environmental damage. A study of the Delaware River concluded that only very moderate shadow prices for recreation (e.g., if a days boating was worth as much as $2.55) were needed to justify the costs of cleaning up the river.[54] Fishing rights might be valued by surrogate valuation or by actual outlay costs when these can be determined—as in the case of the 1961 sale of fishing rights along 1¼ miles of the River Lune in England for £20,750.[55]

---

51 Sanford Rose, "The Economics of Environmental Quality," *Ecology and Economics: Controlling Pollution in the 70's*, Marshall I. Goldman, Ed., (Englewood Cliffs: Prentice-Hall Inc., 1972), p. 23.

52 Allen V. Kneese, "Water Quality Management by Regional Authorities in the Ruhr Area," in *Controlling Pollution: The Economics of a Cleaner America,* Marshall I. Goldman, Ed., (Englewood Cliffs: Prentice-Hall, Inc., 1967), pp. 109–129.

53 Kapp, *op. cit.,* p. 86.

54 Rose, *op. cit.*

55 James A. Crutchfield, "Valuation of Fishing Resources," *Land Economics,* May 1962, pp. 145–154.

Individual studies of the cost of environmental damage can be quite expensive; for this reason alone we should try to learn from and build on work done by others. It would be most helpful if "standard" costs were available for different categories of damage, in different magnitudes and different geographical areas. Obviously such "standards" do not exist, but prior studies can often provide us with usable guidelines and partial estimates that can then be tailored to our circumstances. One of the best studies available is the U.S. Environmental Protection Agency's *Cost of Air Pollution Damage*,[56] which presents 1968 estimates for emissions and costs of pollutants, based on analysis and synthesis of many other studies. The cost estimates include additional costs of health care and impairment of human resources, reduction in residential property values, degradation of materials, and damage to vegetation and agricultural productivity. These estimates permit the cost per pound calculations (1968 figures) shown in Exhibit 5-8. Calculations of this sort, with costs adjusted for inflation, were used by Alexander and Livingstone to estimate the cost of air pollution generated by a particular utility plant.[57] Similarly, Dienemann and Lago describe the use of previously estimated percentage effects of noise increases on property values to evaluate different possible transportation systems for the United States' Northeast Corridor.[58]

Only a limited number of environmental damage measurement cases have been presented, and these are only briefly described. To adequately survey the work that has already been done in this area would more than fill this book. The reader is urged to consult the original sources cited along with the continuing publications of the U.S. Environmental Protection Agency for additional data that might be adapted for use by a particular company.

Public Services and Facilities Used

In using public services and public facilities at all levels, organizations and individuals place a burden on society as a whole—a social cost. Of course this cost is met by individual entities in society largely through the payment of taxes. Thus the question that must be asked about an entity in evaluating this

---

56 Barrett and Waddell, *op. cit.*

57 Michael O. Alexander and J. Leslie Livingstone, "What Are the Real Costs and Benefits of Producing Clean Electric Power?" *Public Utilities Fortnightly,* August 30, 1973, pp. 15–19.

58 Paul F. Dienemann and Armando M. Lago, "Environmental and Social Costs Impacts of Northeast Corridor Transportation System Techniques," in *Benefit Cost Analysis 1971, op. cit.,* pp. 423–449.

EXHIBIT 5-8

Pollutant	Estimated National Cost[59]	Estimated Nationwide Emissions (tons)[60]	Calculated Cost per Pound of Emission
Sulfur oxides	$8,295,000,000	33,200,000	$0.1249
Particulates	5,878,000,000	28,300,000	0.1039
Nitrogen oxides	772,000,000	20,600,000	0.0187

social cost is: What burden does it place on society through its consumption of public services and use of public facilities?

Conceptually we could approach this problem by first enumerating, at least within broad classes, the services and facilities provided by various levels of government—police and fire protection, securities regulation, roads and high-ways, regulation of airways, national defense, the administrative function, and so forth. Use of these services and facilities would then be apportioned among mutually exclusive groups of users, and finally further apportioned within groups to specific entities. The proportions thus developed for, say, the XYZ Company could then be applied to local, state, and national budgets to estimate the company's share of the total cost of government.

This conceptual approach is of course completely impractical at the present time. Perhaps the most practical alternative is to adopt the rather unattractive assumption that total taxes paid are reasonably reflective of the cost of services and facilities used, and then to adjust this total for excessive or less than normal usage in selected areas. A jewelry store, for example, might impose a greater police protection burden on local government because of the nature of its opera-tions and products; a broker might require less than normal police protection but would benefit abnormally from securities regulation.

Abt Associates, Inc., used a variation of this approach in their "social audit." To find the social cost of federal and state services used, total federal and state tax collections were multiplied by the ratio of company revenues to total federal and state corporate revenues. Assuming that *local* services consumed are proportionate to the number of people involved, the company's share of the cost of these services was estimated by multiplying total local taxes by the ratio of "company population" to total local population; the result was reduced by the percentage of the local budget devoted to education on the

59 Barrett and Waddell, *op. cit.,* p. 59.
60 *Ibid.* p. 61.

grounds that Abt Associates Inc., did not use this particular service.[61] Although we might disagree with the specific assumptions made by Abt, its approach is certainly worth consideration.

This approach cannot be directly used for not-for-profit entities, since they do not generally pay taxes. One solution, again based on the less than satisfactory assumption that consumption of services is proportionate to taxes paid, is to develop a surrogate estimate of taxes the entity would have paid had it been profit seeking, and then use this as a rough estimate of the cost of public services and facilities used. In the social benefits and costs assessment of Wichita State University referred to earlier, estimates were made of the total income, property, excise, and sales taxes the University would have paid if it had been a profit-seeking enterprise; the total was taken as a surrogate estimate of the cost imposed on society for public services and facilities used.

The cost of public services and facilities used is difficult—probably impossible—to estimate directly given the present state of social accounting. A surrogate estimate such as those described, while less than totally satisfactory, serves better than ignoring the cost completely.

SUMMARY

The key to social accounting is measurement. The most elegant models are only intellectual curiosities if we do not possess the means to assign reasonably valid and reliable numbers to the model components. For this reason, we have dealt at some length with measurement approaches in this chapter. The objective has *not* been to provide a cookbook layout of precise procedures to follow in each measurement situation; rather the intent has been to provide a taste, a feeling for, the possible approaches. Nor were the cases and examples meant to be exhaustive; again the idea was to show how others had tackled and resolved each problem.

Each entity has a different set of measurement problems characterized by different circumstances. Consequently, social accountants must continue to develop original and ad hoc approaches to the estimation of specific social benefits and costs.

The general approaches described in this chapter—surrogate evaluation, survey techniques, restoration or avoidance cost, appraisals, court decisions,

---

61 *Abt Associates Inc. Annual Report + Social Audit 1973* (Cambridge: Abt Associates Inc., 1974), p. 26.

analysis, and outlay cost—should provide an adequate set of choices for virtually any social measurement problem. They must be used with caution and intelligence, however, in full recognition of their respective weaknesses and especially with careful attention to the attributes we are ultimately trying to measure.

Finally, this discussion of social measurement must be recognized for the interim work that it is. The state of the art should advance dramatically within the next decade. During that period new measurement techniques will be discovered and tested, industrywide and national norms and standards may be developed, and more and more knowledge will become available to guide the social accountant. As far as we have come, we are only on the threshold.

It shall be a vexation only to understand the report.

Isaiah, *XXVIII, 19*

6 Standards for Corporate Social Reporting

Earlier chapters considered present and proposed approaches to social accounting. These proposals and reporting efforts follow no consistent pattern; collectively they appear to have little in common beyond some orientation toward "social" concerns. This is not surprising, for there are presently no articulated objectives for social reporting, no standards or criteria, no "generally accepted" procedures, and no regulatory or professional body directly concerned with social reporting.

In this chapter a dominant objective and tentative standards are proposed for social reporting. Obviously these are not final answers, but are offered as a tentative framework within which the inevitable extensions of present social reporting efforts can occur. Perhaps we can reverse the evolutionary path taken by corporate financial reporting, in which critical attention was first given to procedures and techniques (in the Accounting Research Bulletins of the AICPA's Committee on Accounting Procedure and later in its Accounting Principles Board's opinions); followed by a statement suggesting standards and criteria (in *Statement of the Accounting Principles Board No. 4*); finally leading to an unofficial articulation of objectives (in *Objectives of Financial Statements* by the AICPA's Study Group on the Objectives of Financial Statements).

OBJECTIVES OF CORPORATE SOCIAL REPORTING

Corporate financial reporting has suffered from a lack of clearly specified objectives, and this has resulted in any number of conflicts over reporting alternatives. The Seaview Symposium, for example, matched advocates of a steward-

150

ship objective (financial statements should report on the stewardship of corporate resources) against usefulness partisans (financial statements should provide useful information to investors and others).[1] The stewardship objective would lead to the exclusive use of historical costs, while a usefulness objective would probably lead to the choice of current or fair values. The accounting profession has had a difficult time reaching agreement over financial reporting alternatives largely because there is such a lack of agreement as to the fundamental objective.

Consequently, if any consensus is ever to be reached on social reporting formats and methods, we must first consider the objectives of social reporting. We might think in terms of *corporate* objectives and *social* objectives.

Social reporting might contribute to at least three corporate objectives: public image, learning, and social responsibility. Improved public image might be sought for greater product acceptance, name identification, and avoidance of confrontations (including legal actions, disruption of stockholder meetings, strikes, and boycotts). Management of a corporation might undertake preparation of a social report to see what it could learn about the organization, both internally and in terms of its impact on society. And of course social reports may be issued because of a feeling of social responsibility within the organization—an attitude that society should be informed fully of the corporation's behavior and impact. This last corporate objective appears to be more consonant with the following social objectives.

Social objectives appear to present the same dichotomy encountered for financial reporting: usefulness and stewardship. It can be argued that social reports should be designed primarily to provide useful information—to permit improved allocations of society's resources among organizations, for example. Or it might be asserted that the corporation should report on its stewardship of the resources entrusted to it by society—to permit, for example, identification of noncompliance with social norms (including laws, pollution standards, equality of opportunity, etc.).

Most of the time these objectives may be perfectly compatible, but occasions will arise when pursuit of two different objectives will require two different reporting treatments. To avoid this conflict, we should seek agreement on one *dominant* objective.

Acceptance of one of the corporate objectives as dominant would permit reports that were self-serving; such abuses might (or might not) be rare, but they could still occur. Social reports should be useful, of course, but we do not

---

1 *Corporate Financial Reporting: Conflicts and Challenges,* AICPA, 1969.

know enough at present about the decision models, desires, or even composition of the various audiences to accept this as the dominant objective. Thus, *stewardship reporting* is proposed as the dominant objective, at least during the present developmental stage of social reporting. Reporting on the stewardship of society's resources will serve society but will not require heroic assumptions as to the information needs of the report users.

STANDARDS FOR CORPORATE SOCIAL REPORTING[2]

Proposals for social reporting differ markedly from one another largely because corporate social reporting is in an embryonic stage. Acceptance of standards would narrow the range of differences, but it would be unfortunate if such standards inhibited experimentation. The proposed standards that follow are tentative and intended to serve only during a "development era."

Three standards are proposed. These are viewed as obligatory; reports not complying with all three should be viewed as unacceptable. Related to each standard are secondary critera. These should be viewed as desirable but not essential; nevertheless, noncompliance with secondary criteria should be justified in each instance. Additional reporting considerations are also presented. These may or may not be attainable or even desirable in a given reporting instance, but they should at least be considered. The standards, secondary critera, and additional considerations apply to corporate social reports whether prepared for external dissemination or for internal use only.

Standard No. 1: Relevance

Both the AICPA[3] and the AAA[4] list relevance first among their standards for financial reporting, and it would appear to deserve the same preeminence for social reporting. Corporations should report only that social information which bears on some need or interest in society. Relevant information will generally be useful, but it need not be; some relevant information may only be interest-

---

2 In developing these tentative standards, I was influenced by three sources in particular: *A Statement of Basic Accounting Theory,* American Accounting Association, 1966; *Statement of the Accounting Principles Board No. 4,* AICPA, 1970; and Howard J. Snavely, "Accounting Information Criteria," *The Accounting Review,* April 1967, pp. 223–232.

3 *Statement of the Accounting Principles Board No. 4,* p. 10.

4 *A Statement of Basic Accounting Theory,* p. 7.

ing. The standard of relevance is essentially exclusive in that it dictates that certain information should not be included in social reports, but it also has an inclusive aspect: the more relevant information is to society's needs and interests, the stronger the argument for reporting it.

Secondary Criterion.   Related to the standard of relevance is the secondary criterion of *timeliness*. Information regarding social effects becomes less relevant as the effects recede in time; thus maximum timeliness should be sought in social reporting. Since dated information may be better than no information, however, timeliness is not an obligatory condition and is thus not presented as a standard.

Additional Considerations.   Information to be reported should also be evaluated in terms of its *significance*. Efforts should be made to avoid the reporting of insignificant information. The difficulty here is that, at present, we are not in a very good position to judge what is and what is not significant to every audience of social reports, just as we cannot at present define what is useful to them; thus significance is not proposed as a standard or criterion at this time. Consideration should also be given to *localization* of social reports, or preparation of reports for each community in which the corporation operates, in addition to the total report. Many of the audiences will be concerned only with the effects on and in their community; this information is obscured when a geographically diverse corporation reports only for the total company.

Standard No. 2: Freedom from Bias

The necessity of freedom from bias is indicated by the risk of self-serving and distorted social reporting. There is already too much suspicion, in some cases well deserved, that presently reported information is carefully selected to avoid bad impressions and tends to exaggerate the "good works" or social benefits generated by the corporation. Biased information can be worse than useless; it can be misleading and can result in completely wrong responses. Bias may be intentional or unintentional; both forms must be avoided.

Freedom from bias has several corollaries. Fairness and neutrality mean that social reports do not favor one interest over another. Reliability means that the statements represent what they purport to represent; it is similar to truthfulness, although truth is too imprecise as a standard to guide social reporting. If reported information is sufficiently free from bias, it will also be fair and reliable.

Secondary Criteria.   Three secondary criteria are related to the standard of freedom from bias: *verifiability, independent attestation,* and *completeness.* It is desirable for reported social information to be verifiable; that is, different experts should be able to arrive at essentially the same results. At this stage such a goal may be impracticable; hence verifiability is desirable but not essential.

Any externally reported information benefits from independent attestation, but this is especially true for social reporting, where the risk is unusually great. Unfortunately, the lack of agreement over reporting methods militates against opinion audits on social reports. Perhaps attestation at present must be limited to an expression of opinion as to the reasonableness of assumptions and bases for reporting, similar to the approach used in opinions on financial forecasts.

Completeness is an important but elusive criterion. Obviously *everything* cannot be reported, but critical (and especially derogatory) information should not be omitted. Since we do not know all that might be considered critical by one or another audience, it would be unreasonable to *require* completeness. It should nevertheless be a goal of those associated with social reports, within the limits of their understanding of users' information needs.

Additional Consideration.   *Conservatism* has become somewhat discredited in connection with financial reporting, perhaps because it has been abused. But conservatism should at least be considered in the preparation of social reports, in the sense of avoidance of exaggeration, of public-relations puffery. Consideration should also be given to the *acceptability* of the reports to various audiences; reports that are not believed or trusted will not be useful and will not contribute to society's objectives even if they happen to be completely relia- ble. Finally, consideration should be given to opportunity for *rebuttal.* Readers may disagree with information presented and claims made in social reports. To ensure fairness and acceptance of the reports, provision should perhaps be made at stockholders meetings, in corporate advertisements, and even in social reports themselves for presentation of opposing viewpoints. This adversary con- cept is of course the basis for establishment of facts in court proceedings, and is also reflected in television's fairness doctrine. In fact, the Federal Trade Com- mission is reported to have recently suggested "countercommercials" as responses to misleading television commercials.[5]

---

5 *The New Republic,* June 2, 1973, p. 25.

Standard No. 3: Understandability

Reports that cannot be understood are worthless. There is already some danger that social reporting models will become so complex, so clever, or so obscure that any value will be lost. (This is certainly the case with some of the footnotes now found in financial statements.) Thus understandability is an essential attribute of social reports.

Secondary Criteria. Secondary criteria include *comparability* and *concision*. Intercorporate comparability improves understandability and permits better evaluation. While comparability in social reporting is a desirable goal, it is not universally attainable at present. But we can at least seek comparability of reporting formats, inclusiveness, and measurement techniques within industries.

Concision (or conciseness) suggests selectivity, the omission of trivial and excessive details. The danger is that information overload may occur, resulting in diminished understandability.

Additional Considerations. Intertemporal *consistency* is desirable, but not at the sacrifice of improved reporting models. As reporting models improve, however, reasonable consistency should become a requirement. *Quantifiability* aids understanding and is thus a desirable attribute of reported information, at least when it can be achieved with reasonable reliability. *Monetary expression* may also be desirable since money is about the only understood measure of value in economically developed societies. However, information should not be omitted merely because it cannot be stated in terms of money.

Consideration should also be given to *media propriety*: reports should be presented in language, format, and context understandable to the various audiences; and in media accessible by them. Understanding is also enhanced if reports are presented in a *matching mode* or an *evaluative mode*. The matching mode requires quantification through use of a single metric, and relates positive effects to negative effects, producing some net result (as in the social report proposed in Chapter 4). The evaluative mode presents standards or norms along with actual results for comparison; responsibility reports and budget variance statements are examples from traditional accounting.

EXHIBIT 6-1   Hierarchy of Social Reporting Standards

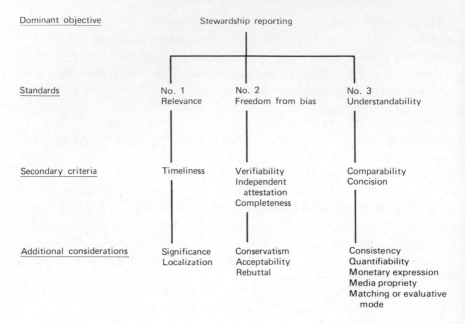

SUMMARY

This chapter considers several possible objectives of social reporting with stewardship reporting identified as presently dominant. Three standards for social reporting—relevance, freedom from bias, and understandability—are proposed, along with several related criteria and additional considerations. Following Snavely,[6] these objectives, standards, criteria, and additional considerations are presented hierarchically in Exhibit 6-1.

As indicated at the outset, these proposals are tentative, and are appropriate only during the present developmental stage of corporate social reporting. As social reporting matures, the objective of usefulness may become dominant. Certainly, attributes such as verifiability and consistency will become more attainable and may move up to the level of standards. But for the present, the proposed standards can perhaps serve as a framework for the more orderly development of social reporting.

---

6 See footnote 2.

One must learn by doing the thing; for
though you think you know it you have not
certainty, until you try.

Sophocles, Trachiniae

7 Now What Are You Going to Do About It?

In a recent study, 46% of responding corporate executives expressed the belief that business firms will be *required* to make a social audit in the future; this percentage increased to 59% for executives in companies with over $10 billion in sales.[1] Some of the comments received with the responses include the following:

> A legal requirement is perhaps unlikely near term. However, other pressures—both internal and external—are likely to result in more social analysis and publication by business.

> If you mean legally required by government action, then—No; if by the consumer market place, then perhaps—Yes.

> The prospect is not only acceptable but I deem it to be necessary. We do not operate in a vacuum. Lou Golden's book *Only by Public Consent* points out the urgency of the situation and should be required reading.

> This is a qualified Yes—the "requirement" may not be greater than the type of EEO, OSHA, and EPA reporting now mandated.

> No way of predicting, but current government regulations make this mandatory in many areas.

> Yes. It's a matter of being responsive to a changing climate of public attitudes and demands, the costs for which will inevitably be reflected in the price for the company's service.

> In the near future—No; longer range—perhaps Yes. Audit itself will not eliminate need to be responsive to society around the business corporation.

---

1 John J. Corson and George A. Steiner, *Measuring Business's Social Performance: The Corporate Social Audit* (Committee for Economic Development, 1974), pp. 36–37.

Pressure is also developing to include social accounting information within the scope of the CPA's external audit; in another recent study, 73% of responding partners in "Big 8" CPA firms were aware of a desire by various groups for their firms to extend their attesting function to include measures (financial and/or nonfinancial) of the effectiveness of social programs.[2] From these responses it is difficult to dismiss social accounting as only a passing fad.

Unfortunately, it's not safe to adopt a wait and see attitude; those companies that are best able to respond to the growing pressures from government and society are those that have already been involved in social accounting for several years. The company that has as yet done nothing may find that further delay will increase the ultimate start-up cost (and disruption) geometrically. The time to (in Ray Bauer's words) "get on the learning curve" is now—yesterday, in fact; certainly not tomorrow or "eventually."

But with all the different proposals, how should a company begin?

The important thing of course is *to* begin. Start small. Keep the initial effort modest while looking down the road. *The first step* is to get top management support. It's not necessary to convince everyone in top management, but it is necessary to obtain enough support for the social accounting effort to provide it with legitimacy. This support must then be communicated throughout the organization—and probably recommunicated from time to time as the effort proceeds. The resistance to revealing sensitive and possibly embarrassing information can be tremendous, even at the lowest levels of an organization; if anything significant is to be accomplished, everyone must understand the company's commitment to the effort. Indeed, even with this commitment, it will sometimes be necessary to go around or outside particular departments and individuals—to patch together estimates without the cooperation of those with the needed information. Of course this resistance will diminish as employees become more knowledgeable about the project and as the threat to their security and authority diminishes.

Early on, one person should be designated to be responsible for reviewing the social accounting literature and keeping current. This person should maintain copies of important reference works, and should be available as the prime source of information on what others are doing in the field. Social accounting is presently in a very dynamic state of development, and important contributions will likely be overlooked in the absence of such continual monitoring.

Next an inventory or enumeration of all social benefits and social costs at-

---

2 AAA Committee on Measures of Effectiveness for Social Programs, "Report of the Committee on Measures of Effectiveness for Social Programs," *The Accounting Review*, Supplement to Vol. XLVII (1972), p. 380.

tributable to the company should be developed. To ensure a complete list, this effort must involve several knowledgeable persons and will most likely be an enlightening exercise in itself. Most of us perceive of our organization's impact on society in the rather narrow context of our own responsibilities. If we are in sales, we don't think much of employment provided or natural resources consumed; if our responsibility is in the manufacturing area, we may be unaware of corporate charitable contributions or of the cost imposed on society for the ultimate disposition of waste resulting from our packaging; if we are in top management, we may not be cognizant of the community and professional activities and donated time of those lower in the organization. Similar examples could be cited ad nauseam, but the point should be clear: several must be involved in this enumeration, and they should represent different functions in the organization.

As the enumeration proceeds, you may also want to identify the major constituencies of your organization. We can always think of customers, stockholders, employees—but you may find that in fact your company serves other constituencies and is indeed quite important to them. A large firm may be not only a major source of employment in a community; it may also provide an important share of school and city tax revenues. Or on the negative side, the firm may impose pollution damage on an area and on citizens who do not benefit in any direct way from the company's presence. If such effects and constituencies seem obvious, it should be noted that they often become obvious only after conscious attention has been directed toward identifying them. To assume complete awareness of all effects in the absence of such a conscious effort may be naive—even arrogant.

Following the enumeration of all social benefits and social costs attributable to the company, you are ready to start assigning measurement numbers. Don't be frustrated by the magnitude of the effort or the difficulty in quantifying certain effects. Remember to always proceed in manageably small steps and to consider each effort as a learning experience and as progress toward a complete and integrated social accounting—but not the final accounting itself. With this sort of approach, you should find that satisfactory estimates of most of your firm's social benefits and costs can be obtained with limited effort, and with each cycle progress can be made in improving the reliability of estimates of the more intractable effects. A patient approach of this sort will yield immediately useful results that can be built on and steadily improved until a complete social accounting is achieved.

An alternative to the complete enumeration and quantification of social benefits and costs is to identify those "social responsibility" activities of the firm—those activities that are expected to cost more than they return to the company—and then assign costs to these. Even this enumeration will be informative in larger organizations where top management cannot be aware of all social responsibility activities and programs in the absence of a specific reporting mechanism.

The costing process will produce the usual problems of allocation; it is suggested that only incremental costs be assigned to the social responsibility programs since the objective is to determine the differential and avoidable cost of each program to the company, and not the full cost in a profit-matching sense. The report of firmwide social responsibility costs should be a useful planning and decision-making instrument, for it will highlight areas of significant omission in the firm's overall program as well as "pet" projects of individual managers whose costs are out of proportion to other programs. For example, it might be discovered that costs of support for a prestigious private university, the alma mater of several managers, far exceeds the costs of a more productive program of aid to minority business managers in the inner city of the company's headquarters community.

A firm's social accounting effort can be expected to produce more reliable and lasting results if it relies on company staff throughout; the initial knowledge of firm operations and structure will save time, the image of a lasting firmwide commitment will be enhanced, and the experience gained will be retained internally. Nevertheless, outside consultants can make a valuable contribution and in some cases may be necessary to get some start in social accounting. Carefully chosen (which means research into the consultant's background and prior experience beyond his or her promotional literature, and ideally some inquiry to former social accounting clients), a consultant can bring to the effort a thorough knowledge of the current state of the art and of measurement approaches, can sometimes overcome internal political squabbles merely by being an outsider, and can ensure a continuing drive toward a previously specified goal (thus avoiding the occasional tendency for social accounting programs to peter out in the face of more current and apparently pressing demands). One special precaution to observe in dealing with a social accounting consultant is to be sure that the final goals of the effort are set by your company and not dictated by the consultant; the consultant will have good suggestions with respect to achievable goals, but you should pay for what you want done rather than what he or she wants to do. It goes without saying that, if consultants are used, firm personnel should also be assigned to the project to ensure that the experience gained is retained within the company.

Whether the social accounting effort is entirely internal or involves consultants, it is important that attention be continually directed to the need for information system modifications. Regardless of the final results and the reaction to these results, social accounting invariably identifies specific information that should be formally developed and reported on a continuing basis—information that will require changes in the data gathering, processing, and reporting system.

At this time greater attention should be given to developing social accounting reports for internal use rather than for external exposure (and this is the approach presently followed by the majority of companies actively engaged in social accounting). Of course you may want to publicize the fact that you are engaged in a social performance assessment, but your initial results are likely to be too tentative to allow you to be confortable with their external disclosure; an analogy are the budgets and forecasts developed for internal planning and decision-making that may not be sufficiently reliable for publication. *If* any results are released or included in your annual report, don't report only the good. Readers are justifiably suspicious of several pages describing all the good works of a company with no hint of any negative effects—no pollution, accidents, discrimination, etc. And you may find that the response to negative results isn't as bad as might be anticipated. Eastern Gas and Fuel found that its stockholders were more impressed with the company's candor in reporting unsatisfactory results than they were by the rather poor accident and safety record.

This takes you through the first "round" of social accounting for your company. Many suggestions could be offered as to what should be done next, but they would be unnecessary and probably superfluous. If a serious job is done in the first round, there will be an abundance of ideas and proposals for extensions and follow-up. Allow for departures from the original plan as you proceed along the learning curve, but also try to maintain a fair degree of comparability to allow for improved evaluation of future performance.

Social accounting will continue to develop. But the company that waits for a perfected model, completely reliable measures, and generally accepted standards will be waiting too long, and may find itself unprepared for the growing challenges of social accounting and of society in the years to come.

Index

Abt Associates, 44–52, 57, 64, 81, 84–86, 89–90, 120, 125, 135, 147–148
Abt, Clark, 81
Acceptability, 154
Accountants for the Public Interest, 4
Accounting Principles Board, *see* American Institute of Certified Public Accountants
Aesthetic pollution, *see* Pollution
Aetna Life & Casualty, 8
Agribusiness Accountability Project, 4
Air pollution, *see* Pollution
Alcohol, 21, 42, 43
Alexander, Michael O., 146
Allende, President, 55
American Accounting Association, 4, 12, 13, 152
  Committee on Environmental Effects of Organization Behavior, 13, 58–59, 61, 63, 88–90
  Committee on Measurement of Social Costs, 13
  Committee on Measures of Effectiveness for Social Programs, 13, 158
  Committee on Non-Financial Measures of Effectiveness, 13
American Baptist Board of Education and Publication, 7
American Baptist Convention, 7
American Civil Liberties Union, 4
American Electric Power Company, 10
American Institute of Certified Public Accountants, 4, 12, 31, 152
  Accounting Principles Board, 150
    Opinion No. 9, 60
    Statement No. 4, 150, 152n
  Accounting Research Bulletins, 150
  Committee on Accounting Procedure, 150
  Committee on Ecology, 12
  Committee on Social Measurement, 12, 64
  Study Group on the Objectives of Financial Statements, 1, 13, 14, 18, 150

Analysis, 116, 125, 135, 143
Anderson, Jack, 5
Appraisals, 115
Attestation, independent, 154
Avoidance cost, 115, 144

Bank of America, 5, 8, 27–28, 32, 55, 56, 57
Barrett, Larry, 143n, 144n, 146n
Battele Institute, 12
Bauer, Raymond A., 37, 158
Beams, Floyd, 60–61, 88–90
Becker, G., 102n, 132, 134
Bias, freedom from, 153
Bribery, 91, 104
Bunyard, F. L., 143

Caldwell, James C., 31
California CPA Foundation, 12
  Symposium on Measurement of Corporate Social Performance, 8, 10
Cambridge Reports, Inc., 114
Cauthorn, Terry, 37
Central Intelligence Agency, 55
Charitable contributions, 10, 19, 26, 30, 33–37, 39–40, 43, 55–56, 71, 74, 79, 82, 96, 98, 159
Chase, Samuel B., 132n
Chase Manhattan, 32–33
Church Project on U.S. Investments in Southern Africa, 7
Citizens Action Program, 4
Clergy and Laity Concerned, 7
Committee for Economic Development, 23
Common Cause, 4
Community planning and improvement, 20, 30, 35, 39, 40, 43, 55, 56, 159
Comparability, 155
Completeness, 154
Concision, 155
Conservatism, 154
Consistency, 155

Consumer issues, 2, 6, 9, 10, 22, 44
Consumers' surplus, 85, 91, 97, 106, 109–110, 117–122, 124, 130
Corcoran, A. Wayne, 76–80, 88–89
Corporate Accountability Research Group, 4, 5
Corson, John, 23, 24, 29, 37, 52, 108, 157n
Council for Corporate Review, 4
Council on Economic Priorities, 4, 5, 10, 11, 26, 71, 89
Council on Environmental Quality, 144n
Court decisions, 116, 142
CPA Examination, 12, 13
Crime, white-collar, 104
Crutchfield, James A., 145n

Daniel Yankelovich, Inc., 114
Day-care centers, 32, 100
Department of Health, Education and Welfare, 2, 144
Department of Housing & Urban Development, 4
Department of the Interior, 144
Dienemann, Paul F., 146
Dilley, Steven C., 68–75, 80, 89–90
Disadvantaged, hiring and promotion, 30
Discrimination, 59, 91, 96, 101, 132–136, 161
Dorfman, Robert, 113n, 141n
Dreyfus Third Century Fund, 9
Drugs, 21, 31, 42, 43

Eastern Gas and Fuel Associates, 33–38, 161
Economics Research Center, University of Chicago, 133
Education, 20, 24, 32, 35, 38, 39, 43, 55, 74
Employee benefits, 71, 74–75, 96, 99, 122–123
Energy use, 2, 27, 40, 54, 75, 97, 101
Environment, 6, 9, 10, 19, 28, 36, 38, 40, 42, 55, 56, 58–59, 76, 80, 83, 88, 103, 142–146
improvements, 74–75, 83, 96, 100, 127
Environmental Protection Agency, 4, 11, 70, 146, 157
Equal Employment Opportunity Commission, 2, 4, 11, 26, 37, 70, 132, 157
Ernst & Ernst, 29, 30
Erosion, 143
Evaluative mode, 155
Exxon, 7

Federal Communications Commission, 4
Federal Power Commission, 70
Federal Trade Commission, 4, 154
Field Foundation, 7
Financial Analysts Federation, 4, 14
Financial Executives Research Foundation, 14
First National Bank of Minneapolis, 36, 38–41
First National City Bank, 7, 8, 11
First Spectrum Fund, 9
Flamholtz, Eric, 23
Food programs, 20
Ford Foundation, 8
Fraud, 91
Freedom from bias, 153
Friends of the Earth, 4
Fromm, Gary, 141n

Gallagher Report, 24
General Accounting Office, 4
General Electric, 7
General Motors, 5, 54–55
Genossenschaften, 145
Glide Foundation, 7
Golden, Lou, 157
Goldman, Marshall I., 145n
Gunn, Sanford C., 57

Hamilton Beach, 44
Handicapped, 55, 82
Harvard University, 8
Health, occupational, 5, 9, 27, 37, 59, 68, 70–71, 73, 87–88, 96, 102, 136–142
public, 38
services, 20
Housing, 20, 28, 32, 38, 39, 43, 55
Human resource accounting, 23, 84

Institute of Life Insurance, Clearinghouse on Corporate Social Responsibility, 8
Institute of Management Science, 12
Interfaith Center for Corporate Responsibility, 7
Internal Revenue Service, 4
International Business Machines, 31–32
International Telephone and Telegraph, 55
Interstate Commerce Commission, 4
Investor Responsibility Research Center, 4, 8

Jarett, Irwin, 29, 52

Jones, Sidney, 30

Kapp, William K., 141n, 145
Kneese, Allen V., 145n
Knievel, Evel, 140

Lago, Armando M., 146
Lave, L. B., 143–144
Lawyer, Robert E., 143
Leininger, Wayne E., Jr., 76–80, 88–89
Linowes, David F., 80–81, 89–90
Livingstone, John Leslie, 57, 146
Localization, 153
Lockheed Aircraft, 2, 91

Marlin, Alice Tepper, 5, 10
Marlin, John Tepper, 64–68, 70, 88–89
Matching mode, 155
Maynard, Betty J., 135n
Military production, 6, 7, 10, 26
Minorities, hiring and promotion, 2, 5–6,
    8–10, 14, 20, 24, 25–26, 32–37,
    39, 41–42, 56, 68, 70–71, 73, 82,
    87, 97, 101, 105, 132–136
Minority business, 20, 25, 26, 27, 32, 40,
    43, 100, 126, 160
Minority Enterprise Small Business Invest-
    ment Company, 55
Mishan, E. J., 119n
Mock, Ruth P., 113n
Monetary expression, 155
Morgan Guaranty Trust, 8
Myers, Sumner, 113n

NAACP, 4
Nader, Ralph 5, 11
National Affiliation of Concerned Business
    Students, 4
National Alliance of Businessmen, 42, 100
National Association of Accountants, 4
    Committee on Accounting for Corporate
    Social Performance, 14, 15–22
National Council of Churches, Corporate
    Information Center, 6
National Federation of Priests' Councils, 7
National Highway Traffic Safety Adminis-
    tration, 141
National Safety Council, 141
Needles, Belverd E., 31
Nelson, J. R., 132n
Nixon, Richard M., 55

Noise pollution, *see* Pollution
Nowlan, Stephan, 11

Occupational Safety and Health Act, 2, 11,
    43, 53, 70, 73, 138, 157
Oil, Chemical and Atomic Workers, 5
Opportunity cost, 28
Ostberg, Henry, 113n
Outlay cost, 116

Pan Am, 2
Pax World Fund, 9
Penn Central, 2, 91
Pensions, 33, 34, 36, 37
Phillips Metallurgical, Inc., 53
Phillips Screw Company, 52–53, 57
Pittston Company, 7
Political contributions, 2, 8, 10
Pollution, 2, 5, 14, 19, 24, 26, 31–32, 38,
    54, 55, 60, 63–68, 77, 84–85, 88,
    91, 104, 106, 159, 161
  aesthetic, 21, 30, 96, 103, 143, 145
  air, 18, 21, 30, 42, 53, 56, 61, 70–71, 75,
    79, 87, 96–98, 103–106, 128, 142–
    144
  audit, 52
  noise, 21, 53, 75, 91, 96, 98n, 103, 110,
    128, 143–144
  solid waste, 21, 27, 53, 63, 79, 96, 98n,
    104, 144, 159
  water, 21, 30, 42–43, 53, 56, 61, 72, 79,
    87, 96, 103, 128, 143–146
Privacy, 32
Producers' surplus, 101, 129–131
Project on Corporate Responsibility, 4
Projective technique, 112
Psychic benefits, 125–126, 131
Public Citizen, Inc., 4
Public Communication, Inc., 4, 12

Quaker Oats, 5, 31, 56
Quantifiability, 155

Reagan, Barbara B., 135n
Rebuttal, 154
Recycling, 40, 56, 77–79, 98n, 103
Reede, A. H., 140–141
Relevance, 152
Research, 22, 54
Resource Planning Association, 53
Restoration cost, 115

Ridker, Ronald G., 140, 143
Roper, E., 132
Rose, Sanford, 145n
Ross, Gerald H. B., 124n
Rutgers University, 135

Safety, occupational, 7, 9, 27, 30, 33, 34,
    36, 37, 56, 59, 68, 70–71, 73, 80,
    82, 88, 96, 102, 136–142, 144, 161
  product, 14, 22, 54, 59, 80, 82–83, 87,
    104
  public, 38, 39, 43
San Francisco Consumer Action, 4
Scovill Manufacturing, 41–44, 57
Seaview Symposium, 150–151
Securities and Exchange Commission, 4, 9, 10
Seidler, Lee J., 64, 86–90, 95
Seskin, E. P., 143–144
Shadow pricing, 110, 145
Shayon, Diana Russell, 11
Shell Cast Corporation, 53
Shell Oil, 5
Sierra Club, 4
Significance, 153
Smith, Georgina M., 135n
Snavely, Howard J., 152n, 156
Social accounting defined, 3
Social benefit defined, 92
Social cost, defined, 92
Social Dimensions Fund, 9
Social Impact Statement, 96–97
Social resource, defined, 92
South Africa, 7, 8, 25, 26, 54, 55
Southern Illinois University Medical School,
    29
Southern Methodist University, 135
Spectrographs, 10
Spectrum Directors, Inc., 9
Steiner, George, 23, 24, 29, 37, 52, 108, 157n
Stewardship reporting, 152
Stigler, George J., 119n
Strip-mining, 61, 82, 100, 115, 145
Surrogate valuation, 110, 115, 124, 126, 145

Survey techniques, 111, 143
Syracuse University, 143

Tax Action Group, 4
Terrain damage, 96, 100, 103, 115
Timeliness, 153
Touche Ross & Co., 124
Training programs, 20
Transportation, 20, 38, 39, 55
Travelers Insurance, 10
Trueblood Committee, 13
TRW, 25–27, 28, 37

Understandability, 155
United Aircraft, 7
United Church of Christ, Center for Social
    Action, 6
United Fund, 100
United States Steel, 55
United Way, 39

Value, defined, 92
Verifiability, 154
Voting, 39

Waddell, Thomas E., 143n, 144n, 146n
Waste, solid, pollution, see Pollution
Water, consumption, 70, 72, 79
  pollution, see Pollution
Weygandt, Jerry J., 68–75, 80, 89–90
Wichita State University, 120, 122, 126–
    127, 131, 148
Wilderness Society, 4
Williams, Doyle Z., 31
Williams, J. D., 143
Women, hiring and promotion, 2, 5–6,
    8–10, 20, 32, 39, 41–42, 56, 70, 73,
    97, 101, 105, 133–135

Xerox, 5

Yankelovich, 114

Zenz, Nicole, 120–121